POPE FRANCIS

AND THE FUTURE
OF CATHOLICISM
IN THE UNITED STATES

The Challenge of Becoming a Church for the Poor

Published by the
UNIVERSITY OF SAN FRANCISCO PRESS
Joan and Ralph Lane Center
for Catholic Studies and Social Thought

University of San Francisco
2130 Fulton Street
San Francisco, CA 94117-1080
www.usfca.edu/lane-center

Published by the University of San Francisco Press through the Joan and Ralph Lane Center for Catholic Studies and Social Thought of the University of San Francisco.

The Lane Center Series promotes the center's mission to advance the scholarship and application of the Catholic intellectual tradition in the church and society with an emphasis on social concerns. The series features essays by Lane Center scholars, guest speakers, and USF faculty. It serves as a written archive of Lane Center events and programs and allows the work of the center to reach a broader audience.

POPE FRANCIS

AND THE FUTURE OF CATHOLICISM IN THE UNITED STATES

The Challenge of Becoming a Church for the Poor

THE LANE CENTER SERIES

VOLUME 3, FALL 2015

Edited by Erin Brigham,
David E. DeCosse, and Michael Duffy

 UNIVERSITY OF SAN FRANCISCO | Joan and Ralph Lane Center for Catholic Studies and Social Thought

TABLE OF CONTENTS

TABLE OF CONTENTS (CONT.)

POPE FRANCIS AND THE FUTURE OF CATHOLICISM IN THE UNITED STATES: THE CHALLENGE OF BECOMING A CHURCH FOR THE POOR

INTRODUCTION

ERIN BRIGHAM, DAVID E. DECOSSE, AND MICHAEL DUFFY, EDITORS

"A Church for the Poor" by then-auxiliary bishop of San Francisco, Robert W. McElroy, was published in *America Magazine* on Oct. 21, 2013. In it, McElroy, now the bishop of San Diego, challenges the

---

Erin Brigham is the Coordinator of Research for the Joan and Ralph Lane Center for Catholic Studies and Social Thought at the University of San Francisco, where she also teaches in the areas of Catholic theology and ethics. Her published works include: *See, Judge, Act: Catholic Social Teaching and Service Learning* (Anselm Academic, 2013) and *Sustaining the Hope for Unity: Ecumenical Dialogue in a Postmodern World* (Liturgical Press, 2012).

David E. DeCosse is the Director of Campus Ethics Programs at the Markkula Center for Applied Ethics at Santa Clara University, where he is also Adjunct Associate Professor of Religious Studies. He has written for academic journals like *Theological Studies* and journalistic outlets like *National Catholic Reporter*. With Kristin Heyer, he co-edited the book *Conscience and Catholicism: Rights, Responsibilities, and Institutional Responses* (Orbis 2015).

Michael Duffy is the Director of the Joan and Ralph Lane Center for Catholic Studies and Social Thought and the Interim Director of the Institute for Catholic Educational Leadership (ICEL). Dr. Duffy teaches as an adjunct faculty with the Catholic Educational Leadership degree programs and is an alumnus of ICEL, having received his doctorate in 2005. His dissertation was titled, "Directives within Catholic Social Thought for the Promotion of Justice through Educational Activities." He is also co-chair of USF's University Council for Jesuit Mission and serves on the national steering committee of the Commitment to Justice in Jesuit Higher Education conference as well as the executive board of Catholic Scholars for Worker Justice.

American Catholic Church to see more deeply what Pope Francis is asking for when he calls the Catholic Church to be a church for the poor.

Bishop McElroy, who held the Lane Center's Anna and Joseph Lo Schiavo Chair in Catholic Studies at the University of San Francisco for six months in 2008, generated significant discussion with his article. Following conversations with colleagues at Santa Clara University, the Jesuit School of Theology of Santa Clara University, and Faith in Public Life, the Lane Center pulled together a roundtable of scholars, activists, and religious leaders to meet with Bishop McElroy and discuss how best to support his challenge, engage the Catholic intellectual tradition, and transform the public political conversation across the western United States and the rest of the country.

On April 4, 2014, 20 participants, including Bishop McElroy and the authors in this volume, met on the campus of the University of San Francisco for a daylong gathering centered on the issue of poverty and the task of getting poverty back on the political agenda for the American Catholic Church. John Gehring of the Baltimore-based group Faith in Public Life presented findings from a 2013 study he conducted on the church in the public area and contemporary society in a report titled, "Be Not Afraid."[1] Bishop McElroy outlined how his article, "A Church for the Poor," developed and evolved. The conversation that followed centered on how we might assist in putting poverty and economic justice back on the agenda for the church in the United States and around the world. Throughout the day, participants shared relevant scholarship, as well as stories of people with whom they have worked, campaigns undertaken by organizations, and struggles they had encountered for a deeper and broader understanding and articulation of the Catholic social tradition.

Bishop McElroy summed up well in his article what many participants were expressing,

> Both the substance and methodology of Pope Francis' teachings on the rights of the poor have enormous implications for the culture and politics of the United States and for the church in this country. These teachings demand a transformation of the existing Catholic political

conversation in our nation, a transformation reflecting three themes: prioritizing the issue of poverty, focusing not only on intrinsic evils but also on structural sin, and acting with prudence when applying Catholic moral principles to specific legal enactments.[2]

One of the strategies the roundtable generated was a series of essays on these very issues. The group envisioned a volume that would present voices and perspectives in support of the message of Bishop McElroy and in support of the larger call from Pope Francis. The participants insisted upon writings that would be accessible to a broad audience of the American Catholic community and others who have resonated with Francis' message. The resulting volume supports Bishop McElroy's call from multiple perspectives.

The first part of this volume locates McElroy's article in the historical and theological context of the U.S. Catholic Church. By highlighting some of the ecclesial and political realities that have shaped the public voice of U.S. Catholicism, the first four essays reinforce the significance of Bishop McElroy's insistence on becoming a church for the poor. Perhaps nothing reinforces the relevance of this invitation more than stories from community organizers and activists working alongside the poor and marginalized, which the subsequent three essays feature.

Following Pope Francis, Bishop McElroy invites the U.S. Catholic Church to rediscover the consistent ethic of life—a tradition that recognizes the interconnectedness of moral issues related to human life and dignity. This is essential if the U.S. bishops are to lead the Catholic Church into becoming a church for the poor, John Gehring argues in his essay, "The Francis Effect: A Better Catholic Values Debate in American Public Life?" Gehring, who is the Catholic program director for Faith in Public Life, presents a historical overview of the U.S. bishops' involvement in politics, which he characterizes currently as entrenched in a conservative political agenda. This agenda prioritizes certain moral issues over the full breadth of concerns that threaten human dignity. Embracing the consistent ethic of life, Gehring argues, will allow the church to reclaim its public significance in the United States. Furthermore, it is in line with Pope Francis' vision for the church, a point argued by John Coleman in his essay, "Pope Francis and the Consistent Ethic of Life." Coleman, an expert on the Catholic social tradition, summarizes Pope Francis' writings, which delineate clear linkages between various life issues—the death penalty, abortion, torture, human trafficking, and poverty.

Pope Francis' challenge to overcome the selective focus on abortion and same-sex marriage in order to fight poverty has been embraced by many Americans who have been disillusioned with the Catholic Church. As the number of people who do not affiliate with organized religion rises in this country, polls have shown that many Americans fault religious leaders who narrowly align themselves with conservative politics. Pope Francis' theological understanding of the church speaks to this context, Erin Brigham argues in "The Church as a Field Hospital: The Ecclesiology of Pope Francis." The image of the church as a field hospital challenges Catholics to engage deeply with the wounds of society, stepping out of their comfort zones to be transformed by the poor and the outcast. Expanding the moral discourse among U.S. Catholics to include social issues such as poverty invites a reconsideration of how the concept of intrinsic evil functions to prioritize certain issues over others. Ethicist William O'Neill unpacks this concept in "Intrinsic Evil—A Guide for the Perplexed." Echoing McElroy, O'Neill demonstrates why structural evils such as poverty can be just as grave as intrinsic evils because realities engendered by poverty violate the very dignity of the human person.

The field hospital church—a church informed by the experiences of the poor and oppressed—is made visible by community organizers and activists informed by the Catholic social tradition. John Baumann, founding director of PICO (People Improving Communities through Organizing), writes about the significance of Pope Francis' field hospital church in the context of faith-based community organizing in "Confronting the 'Economy of Exclusion' from the Ground Up." Baumann identifies parallels between PICO and Pope Francis in their approach to empowering the poor through accompaniment. This approach models the kind of solidarity called for in the Catholic social tradition, a point reinforced by PICO organizer Joseph Fleming in "Solidarity and Community Organizing." Through concrete stories of effective community organizing, Fleming distinguishes between shallow talk of solidarity and the kind of solidarity that bridges communities once separated by imbalances of power.

Like the Baumann and Fleming essays, the essay by Adriana Guzmán, Lorena Melgarejo, and Luis Enrique Bazán is rooted in concrete experience. In "Latino Immigration, Faith, and Community Organizing: The San Francisco Experience," the three reflect on their own work as community organizers and advocates in vibrant and vulnerable Latin American immigrant communities. Here, the reality of structural sin that Bishop McElroy invites us to consider is experienced in the poverty that drives migrants to come to El Norte and in the many challenges faced on arrival.

Lisa Fullam's essay, "Pope Francis, Women, and the Church for the Poor," addresses a vexing challenge: How will it be possible to become the church for the poor while the church continues its discriminatory attitudes and practices toward women who in fact constitute most of the world's poor? Fullam notes—as visionary as Pope Francis has been on many things—he remains locked within a traditional Vatican worldview in which "women are lauded for maternity, not political savvy, for intuition, not intellectual acuity." And such a view, she argues, makes it difficult for the church to appreciate the enduring injustice marking many women's lives.

The essay by Brian Cahill, "Pope Francis, Inclusiveness, and the LGBT Community," explores the theme of becoming a church for the poor through a powerful lens: Cahill's own journey of understanding for his gay son. That paternal journey revealed to him the limits of the church's natural law ethic about homosexuality: The language of "intrinsic disorder" was fundamentally incompatible with what it meant to affirm the inherent goodness of his son. Reinforcing this revelation, as Executive Director of San Francisco Catholic Charities, Cahill witnessed how the same natural law ethic informed the official church's discriminatory and destructive efforts to restrict gay and lesbian couples from adopting foster children, often among the poorest of the poor.

Bishop McElroy's essay notes the need for a deeper engagement with structural sin on the part of American Catholics. Kristin Heyer's essay, "Social Sin, Economic Inequality, and the Common Good," highlights the powerful, complex ways in which sin and structure interact around the issue of economic inequality. Such an issue is never sufficiently addressed in the rarefied categories alone of supply and demand and the cultural baggage such categories carry in tow. Instead, as she puts it: " ...distinct elements of social sin—dehumanizing trends, unjust structures, and harmful ideologies—shape complex dynamics at play in perpetuating inequalities."

While Heyer's essay examines how social sin fosters poverty, Thomas Massaro's essay focuses on a practical issue of power that surely perpetuates poverty in the United States: The restriction of voting rights of the poor themselves. In the last years, legal strategists have devised increasingly sophisticated ways to impose such restrictions—and all of this despite no widespread evidence of voter fraud. So far, the Catholic leadership has not forcefully denounced such restrictions. Massaro's essay, "Voter Suppression as a Priority: Fighting Disenfranchisement (Yet Again)," calls for that to change.

The final essay of the book by David DeCosse examines a fundamental topic underlying the challenge of becoming a church for the poor: The theology of conscience. In "Conscience, Missionary Discipleship, and a Church for the Poor," he argues that the bishops' election year document *Faithful Citizenship* needs to be revised to accommodate the theology of conscience articulated by Pope Francis—a theology more open to prudence and more conducive to the conversion needed to become a church for the poor.

Reflecting the diversity of perspectives at the roundtable gathering nearly two years ago, this volume combines the voices of theologians and activists, ministers and ethicists. Such collaboration, we believe, is crucial for taking on the challenge initiated by Pope Francis and contextualized in the U.S. context by Bishop McElroy because becoming the church of the poor and for the poor necessitates multiple levels of transformation—political, moral, theological, and personal.

1   The report is available online at http://www.faithinpubliclife.org/wp-content/uploads/2013/06/FPL-CCHD-report.pdf.

2   Robert McElroy, "A Church for the Poor," in *America* magazine (October 21, 2013).

THE FRANCIS EFFECT: A BETTER CATHOLIC VALUES DEBATE IN AMERICAN PUBLIC LIFE?

John Gehring

Pope Francis is shaking up the Roman Catholic Church with an ambitious project of spiritual renewal and structural reform. In place of a self-referential culture of clericalism, the first Jesuit pope and the first to take his name from the *poverello* of Assisi wants a "poor church for the poor" that steps out of the security of the sanctuary into the messy uncertainty of the streets. By appointing bishops who share this vision and exploring systemic ways to decentralize power away from Rome, Pope Francis is renewing the commitments that shaped the Second Vatican Council. Reform, of course, is in the eye of the beholder. What many cheer as a new springtime for the church, others endure impatiently as "a temporary cold spell," as German Cardinal Walter Kasper, often called the "pope's theologian," evocatively phrased it during a 2014 speech at the Catholic University of America in Washington.[1]

John Gehring is Catholic program director at Faith in Public Life, an advocacy group in Washington. He is the author of *The Francis Effect: A Radical Pope's Challenge to the American Catholic Church*, (Lanham, MD: Rowman & Littlefield, August 2015).

Even as the Francis papacy shifts the internal power dynamics of the church, the papacy also has the potential to help breathe new life into a Catholic political narrative in the United States that, in recent decades, has been narrowly framed, out of balance, and driven by drearily predictable culture wars. An American hierarchy once known for laying the moral architecture that led to New Deal reforms in the 1930s and influential national letters on economic justice and nuclear weapons in the 1980s, has of late earned a reputation—fair or not—for being "firmly on the Republican side in American politics," as Archbishop Emeritus John Quinn of San Francisco warned in a 2009 *America* magazine essay.[2] Quinn wrote his essay in the wake of the episcopal furor that erupted when the University of Notre Dame invited President Obama to give a commencement address. How did Catholic identity get reduced to a few hot-button issues? Why did the most strident figures in the U.S. Catholic Church often drown out the sanity caucus?

The remaking of the Catholic political narrative in our country is a story more than four decades in the making and defies simple description. It includes a landmark U.S. Supreme Court ruling on abortion, the towering papacy of John Paul II, a realignment of party politics, seismic cultural shifts in support for gay rights, and a new generation that rose to power at the U.S. bishops' national headquarters in Washington. Along the way, activist Catholics on the right funded think tanks partnered with conservative evangelicals and built influential networks that brought together church leaders, Republican politicians, and wealthy philanthropists in common cause. In stark contrast, progressives in the post-Civil Rights era often mistakenly conceded faith-based advocacy and values debates to a politicized Religious Right movement that damaged the image of faith in the public square.[3]

During the 35 years that Pope John Paul II and Pope Benedict XVI led the Catholic Church, a vocal minority of strident bishops, conservative intellectuals, and culture warriors wielded disproportionate influence in shaping the political voice of Catholicism in the United States. The late Rev. Richard John Neuhaus of *First Things*, George

Weigel of the Ethics and Public Policy Center, Michael Novak of the American Enterprise Institute—and more recently Robert George of Princeton University—filtered church teaching through an ideological prism that baptized the Iraq war, made an idol of unfettered markets, and narrowed Catholic identity to a checklist that aligned neatly with the Republican Party's agenda. These influential Catholic intellectuals, along with more pugnacious commentators like Bill Donohue of the Catholic League, played a key role in the steady erosion of a consistent life ethic championed by the late Cardinal Joseph Bernardin of Chicago. A framework of "non-negotiable" issues began to replace a more expansive pro-life witness that recognizes myriad and interconnected threats to human dignity.

At a Washington conference attended by several American bishops in 2008, Robert George of Princeton—dubbed "The Conservative-Christian Big Thinker" in a *New York Times* magazine profile—advised church leaders that instead of wasting much energy on advocating for living wages for workers, health care reform, and other justice issues central to the common good, they should focus on what he called "the moral social issues"—abortion, marriage, and embryonic stem cell research.[4] "Whenever I venture out into the public square, I would almost invariably check it out with Robby first," Archbishop John Myers of Newark told the magazine, noting that many bishops consider George "the pre-eminent Catholic intellectual."[5]

The distorted political theology favored by Robert George and some vocal American Church leaders who held influence under the previous two papacies, often became the context for Catholic values debates in the media and politics. During the 2004 presidential election, a San-Diego based group, Catholic Answers Action, released *A Voter's Guide for Serious Catholics* that argued Catholics should only vote based on a candidate's position on "five non-negotiable issues": abortion, euthanasia, embryonic stem-cell research, human cloning, and same-sex marriage. Unlike the effects of war, inequality, and poverty, Catholic Answers and some church leaders argued, these were all "intrinsically evil."[6] Ten million copies of the voter's guide were distributed during the campaign.[7]

Pope Francis himself is skeptical of this kind of theological and moral reductionism. "I have never understood the expression non-negotiable values," Pope Francis told the Italian daily *Corriere della Sera* in a 2014 interview. "Values are values, and that is it. I can't say that, of the fingers of a hand, there is one less useful than the rest."[8]

A BRAVE NEW WORLD

U.S. Catholic leaders have an unprecedented opportunity in the Francis era. The clergy sexual abuse scandals, the crass politicization of Communion during past presidential elections, and the hierarchy's high-profile battles with the Obama administration over contraception funding have shaped an image of an American hierarchy that is hunkered down and embattled, more weary and wary than joyful. If bishops need a jolt of energy and inspiration as they search for a more effective public presence, the roadmap is clear. Pope Francis provides a model of pastoral leadership when it comes to prickly issues of sexuality and family, and his focus on structural injustice—what he calls an "economy of exclusion and inequality"— can help rescue American bishops from the dead end street of culture wars.

"Bishops have a lot to learn from Pope Francis," Archbishop Emeritus Joseph Fiorenza, a former president of the U.S. bishops' conference, told me,

> Catholic identity is far broader than opposition to abortion and same-sex marriage. Catholic identity is a commitment to living the Gospel as Jesus proclaimed it, and this must include a commitment to those in poverty.[9]

Fiorenza thinks that conservatives who deflect attention from the pope's bold critique of inequality and those who reduce the church's commitment to building a culture of life to single-issue politics face a real test from the Francis papacy. "The pope is saying we have to oppose abortion but there must be a broader agenda." He went on to say:

Some pro-life advocates don't like to hear that and think if you take the focus off abortion you weaken your position. The pope is saying you weaken your pro-life position when you don't take a broader view of issues that attack human life. Some people think there are only sins that are intrinsic evil, but the pope is saying the economy has built in a structure that strongly impacts against the humanity of people and that is an evil too.[10]

Bishop Robert McElroy is one of several "Francis bishops" who recognize the need for a reboot. Appointed by the pope to lead the San Diego diocese in the spring of 2015, the Stanford and Harvard University graduate is widely respected for his intellectual chops and pastoral style. He was quickly out of the gate after the new pontiff's election, urging his fellow bishops to recognize the ground-shifting moment. "Both the substance and methodology of Pope Francis' teachings on the rights of the poor have enormous implications for the culture and politics of the United States and for the church in this country," he wrote in a 2013 *America* magazine. "These teachings demand a transformation of the existing Catholic political conversation in our nation."[11]

McElroy is not surprised by the pushback Francis is facing from some commentators and clerics. "There is a difference in tone and emphasis that is not merely symbolic," he told me in an interview. "It calls for a change in heart and mind. We're being called to live a different life and that's not easy for any of us." He acknowledges frustration that the U.S. bishops' conference over the last few years has been "consumed with a religious liberty push" and fighting same-sex marriage. "I do think there will be a movement out of a preoccupation with those issues, and an effort to bring poverty front and center. The bishops have the memo from Pope Francis, and we are trying to integrate this into our work in dioceses. It's like a big ship adjusting course. It can't be done all at once."

REVIVING THE CONSISTENT ETHIC OF LIFE

The consistent ethic of life vision emphasized by the late Cardinal Joseph Bernardin is getting a jumpstart under the Francis papacy. If the paradigm of American culture wars divides up issues of family values, economic justice, and abortion along an ideological spectrum that falls into predictable partisan categories, Francis is reviving a robust Catholic tradition that refuses to accept those conventional terms of debate. The pope addresses economic dignity and care for immigrants as sanctity of life issues:

> Just as the commandment 'Thou shalt not kill' sets a clear limit in order to safeguard the value of human life," Pope Francis writes, "today we also have to say 'thou shalt not' to an economy of exclusion and inequality. Such an economy kills.[12]

Cardinal Sean O'Malley of Boston, the pope's top advisor in the United States, echoed that message during his homily before the 2014 March for Life in Washington. The cardinal called poverty a "dehumanizing force" and insisted "the Gospel of Life demands that we work for economic justice in our country and our world."[13] Francis' first trip as pope outside of Rome was to Lampedusa, an island off the coast of Italy where thousands of migrants and refugees from Africa have died at sea trying to enter Europe. There, the pope decried a "globalization of indifference" and the blood on all of our hands.[14] When Cardinal O'Malley led a delegation of bishops to the U.S.-Mexico border to bear witness to the suffering and death caused by our broken immigration system, he called comprehensive immigration reform "another pro-life issue."[15] In the lead up to the national anti-abortion March for Life rally in January of 2015, 100 Catholic leaders—including more than two dozen presidents of Catholic universities and a former pro-life spokeswoman for the U.S. bishops' conference—released a letter that called attention to the deaths of migrants at the border. The letter urged Catholic elected officials to pass comprehensive reform and "defend the sanctity of human lives at all stages." Five dioceses in Southern California held their first "One Life" march, drawing attention to not only abortion but to an array of moral issues including homelessness and the treatment of the elderly. Archbishop José Gomez created the event, according to the archdiocese, in response to Pope Francis' efforts to address a broad spectrum of issues bearing on human life and dignity. More than 10,000 people attended the march in Los Angeles.[16]

IN SEARCH OF COMMON GROUND

When Pope Francis canonized John Paul II and John XXIII a few weeks after Easter in 2014, he sent a message of unity by declaring as saints two men often deployed as symbols for competing Catholic camps. The pope consistently reminds the faithful, even if we find it tough to hear, that the Gospel leaves no room for ideology. He is inconveniently challenging the left and right to step outside of our comfort zones. This is hard, essential work at a time of deep polarization in the church and American politics. Can Catholic progressives and Catholic conservatives find fresh paths forward to heal the wounds in our church, and also forge common ground in the policy arena to address poverty and inequality, help struggling families, support pregnant women, and reduce the number of abortions? In many respects, the answer to that difficult question depends on how American Catholics choose to use the rare gift found in this unexpected moment of renewal and hope for the church.

It's no secret that the Catholic Church is diminished by the tribalism and litmus tests that often define the dysfunctional culture of secular politics. We are too often a church of MSNBC Catholics and Fox News Catholics who reinforce our own narratives and tune out opposing views. We can do better. Catholic Democrats and Catholic Republicans—or those who increasingly feel politically homeless from either party—share a common faith that includes clear teachings about the sanctity of life, a preferential option for the poor, and a commitment to the common good. As the world watches the Catholic Church with new eyes, we must strive for something better than turf wars and dueling talking points. Pope Francis is challenging us to think bigger and build "a church of encounter" that goes to the margins where people are hurting and broken. A navel-gazing church obsessed with internal bickering and settling old scores will not meet that transcendent mission. Catholic liberals and conservatives have been locked in a fierce tug-of-war over Catholic identity for decades—or centuries, depending on how you read it. This conflict often has roots in legitimate disagreements between faithful Catholics who love our church in equal measure, even if we sometimes reach different conclusions. A core challenge will be to move beyond confining labels and acknowledge the "cafeteria Catholicism" that both liberals and conservatives find comforting. Defending life and fighting for social justice should not be viewed as clashing political agendas, but part of the same moral framework for building a just society. When we unravel the strands that weave together the coherence of Catholic teaching, we always risk reducing faith to just another ideology in service of political ends. Instead, Pope Francis challenges our "throw-away culture" that tramples human dignity by treating life in the womb, migrants dying in the desert, the homeless, and forgotten elderly as disposable. In his critique of a "globalization of indifference,"—as the pope describes a culture of comfort and extreme individualism—Catholics across the political spectrum are finding fresh opportunity to reclaim a common good vision that deepens our values debates and moves beyond the stale divisions of the past. A maverick pope is asking us to roll up our sleeves, walk into the mess, and get to work.

1   Vinnie Rotondaro, "Cardinal Kasper- 'Pope Francis Does Not Represent a Liberal Position, but a Radical Position,'" in *National Catholic Reporter* (November 7, 2014), accessed July 24, 2015, http://ncronline.org/news/people/cardinal-kasper-pope-francis-does-not-represent-liberal-position-radical-position.

2   John Quinn, "The Public Duty of Bishops," in *America* magazine (August 31, 2009).

3   I explore these issues at length in my book *The Francis Effect: A Radical Pope's Challenge to the American Catholic Church* (Lanham, MD: Rowman & Littlefield, 2015).

4   David Kirkpatrick, "The Conservative-Christian Big Thinker," in *The New York Times Magazine* (December 16, 2009), accessed July 24, 2015, http://www.nytimes.com/2009/12/20/magazine/20george-t.html?pagewanted=all.

5   Kirkpatrick, "The Conservative-Christian Big Thinker."

6   Catholic Answers, *A Voters' Guide for Serious Catholics* (San Diego: Catholic Answers Press, 2012), accessed July 24, 2015, http://www.catholic.com/sites/

default/files/voters_guide_for_serious_catholics.pdf.

7   Peter Steinfels, "Voters' Guides Define Moral Compromises to Take to the Polls," in *The New York Times* (October 14, 2006), accessed July 24, 2015, http://www.nytimes.com/2006/10/14/us/politics/14beliefs.html.

8   Andrea Gagliarducci, "All Values are Non-Negotiable, Pope Says in a New Interview," *Catholic News Agency* (March 5,2014), accessed July 24, 2015, http://www.catholicnewsagency.com/news/all-values-are-non-negotiable-pope-says-in-new-interview/.

9   Joseph Fiorenza as quoted from an interview with the author.

10   Ibid.

11   Robert McElroy, "A Church for the Poor," in *America* magazine (October 21, 2013).

12   Pope Francis, Apostolic Exhortation on the Proclamation of the Gospel in Today's World, *Evangelii Gaudium* (2013), 53.

13   Sean Michael Winters, "Cardinal O'Malley's Sermon," in *National Catholic Reporter* (January 22, 2014), accessed July 24, 2015, http://ncronline.org/blogs/distinctly-catholic/cardinal-omalleys-sermon.

14   Pope Francis, Homily during his visit to Lampedusa, (July 8, 2013), accessed July 24, 2015, http://w2.vatican.va/content/francesco/en/homilies/2013/documents/papa-francesco_20130708_omelia-lampedusa.html.

15   John Allen, "O'Malley Preaches Support for Immigrants at US Border," in *The Boston Globe* (April 2, 2014), accessed July 24, 2015, http://www.bostonglobe.com/metro/2014/04/01/cardinal/qVnbOwt2RE3Imym9P52JoL/story.html.

16   Michelle Boorstein, "Abortion Opponents Rally on Mall, Optimistic that Nation's Views are Aligning with Theirs," in *The Washington Post* (January 22, 2015), accessed July 24, 2015, http://www.washingtonpost.com/local/under-pope-francis-american-catholics-see-the-pro-life-label-as-broader-than-abortion/2015/01/22/621671dc-a1a7-11e4-b146-577832eafcb4_story.html.

POPE FRANCIS AND THE CONSISTENT ETHIC OF LIFE

JOHN COLEMAN, S.J.

The term, "the consistent ethic of life" was coined by Cardinal Joseph Bernardin in his first lecture on the topic at Fordham University in 1983. He stated, "I am convinced that the pro-life position of the Church must be developed in terms of a comprehensive and consistent ethic of life." He wanted to shape a position of linkage among various life issues. He referred to this ethic as "a seamless garment."[1] Bernardin analyzed a spectrum of life issues beyond war and abortion, affirming a linkage between issues such as the death penalty, euthanasia, poverty, and welfare reform, health care, and civil rights. As he said, "The theological foundation of the consistent ethic of life is the defense of the person."[2] Bernardin wished to initiate a dialogue in the church and within public life. Following this intention, he requested that arguments and differences of opinion be voiced with charity and civility.[3]

To meet the criticisms of those who thought the church should focus on abortion and not dilute this most crucial pro-life issue, Bernardin explained that, of course, a foundational consistent ethic of life must sometimes take account of distinctions between various life issues;

John A. Coleman S.J. is associate pastor at Saint Ignatius Parish, San Francisco. He is also the Casassa Professor of Social Values, Emeritus from Loyola Marymount University, Los Angeles. Coleman has written or edited 16 books and contributed many chapters to other books.

however, one must not break the consistent linkage among them.[4] After all, extreme poverty leading to malnutrition or lack of adequate medicine also shortens lives and causes death. Poverty also increases abortion. Critics of Bernardin, such as George Weigel who opposed the consistent ethic of life, talked about the priority of "intrinsic evils." He argued that intrinsic evils such as murder, genocide, abortion, euthanasia, racism, torture, and suicide always took priority over all other issues such as war, poverty, unjust immigration laws (which, in his view, were optional).[5] It is worth noting, however, that some structural issues such as extreme poverty may actually threaten more lives than one intrinsic evil such as abortion or adultery.

Several authors observe Pope Francis as espousing something similar to Bernardin's consistent ethic of life, although he does not explicitly use the term. Bishop Robert W. McElroy, in "A Church for the Poor"—an essay which gave rise to this volume—cites Francis. He calls for three crucial priorities: "Prioritizing the issue of poverty; focusing not only on intrinsic evils but also on structural sin; and acting with prudence when applying Catholic moral principles to specific legal enactments."[6] Key for McElroy is the concept of the core dignity of the human person. "Both abortion and poverty, each in its own way and to its own degree constitute an assault on the very core dignity of the human person."[7] Addressing such an entrenched structural evil as poverty, which Pope Francis often does, is neither optional nor secondary. As McElroy puts it,

> We are called to see the issues of abortion and poverty, marriage and immigrant rights, euthanasia and war, religious liberty and restorative justice not as competing alternatives often set within a partisan framework but as a complementary continuum of life and dignity.[8]

Opponents of Bernardin's consistent ethic of life, such as Richard Neuhaus, George Weigel, and Michael Novak, disagreed with him and the other American Bishops of the 1980s on their teaching about the limits on war and their concern for an economy that fought poverty. These critics also thought that, strategically, the Catholic culture war against "secularism" was better fought if it focused almost exclusively on three or so issues, such as abortion, euthanasia, and gay marriage. They feared a broader consistent ethic of life entailed a surrender to the ambient culture. Some variant of their argument is still heard today. But, as we will see, Pope Francis argues that those who break the link between structural evils and intrinsic evil will never adequately address intrinsic evil.

In an essay entitled "Cardinal Bernardin's Gift to Pope Francis: The Legacy of the 'Consistent Ethic of Life,'" journalist David Gibson notes that there is no real indication that Francis knows the writings of Bernardin, but that the pope's many remarks repeatedly evoke Bernardin's signature teachings on the consistent ethic of life—"The view that church doctrine champions the poor and vulnerable from womb to tomb and on finding 'common ground' to heal divisions in the church."[9] As Gibson puts it,

> Francis, for example, repeatedly stresses economic justice and care for the poor as priorities for Catholics and he warned that the church has become 'obsessed' with a few issues such as abortion, contraception and homosexuality and needs a 'new balance.'[10]

Francis does not waffle in his condemnation of abortion. In a talk he gave to an Italian movement of life, Francis makes this clear,

> Thank you for the testimony you give by promoting and defending human life from the moment of conception. We know it, human life is sacred and inviolable. Every civil right rests on the recognition of the first and fundamental right, that of life, which is not subordinated to any condition, be it quantitative, economic or least of all ideological.[11]

Elsewhere, Francis links this life issue to concerns of poverty and radical inequality:

> Just as the commandment, 'Thou shalt not kill' sets a clear limit in order to safeguard the value of human life, today we also have to say 'thou shalt not' to an economy of exclusion and inequality. Such an economy kills. Human beings are themselves considered consumer goods to be used and then discarded. We have created a 'throw away' culture.[12]

Francis' consistent ethic was already evident in his very choice of name as pope. He noted,

> When the Cardinals elected me as Bishop of Rome and Universal Pastor of the Catholic Church, I chose the name of 'Francis,' a very famous saint who loved God and every human being deeply, to the point of being called 'universal brother.' He loved, helped and served the needy, the sick and the poor; he also cared greatly for creation.[13]

The United States Conference of Catholic Bishops (USCCB) Department of Justice, Peace and Human Development has compiled a helpful 86-page collection of quotes from speeches, messages, homilies, and audiences of Pope Francis. They cover a range of topics such as care for creation; charity/service; the common good; economic justice and inequality; development; food/hunger; life and dignity; labor; migrants and refugees; peace; poverty; simple living; solidarity; and human trafficking. One cannot miss Francis' deep commitment to a consistent ethic of life. I lift up only a few of his statements from this compilation.[14]

Lest one think Francis downplays abortion or euthanasia, he reminds us:

> Human life, the person, is no longer perceived as a primary value to be respected and protected, especially if poor or disabled, if not yet useful— such as the unborn child—or no longer needed—such as the elderly.[15]

Again, he said,

> Among the vulnerable for whom the Church wishes to care with particular love and concern are unborn children, the most defenseless and innocent among us. Nowadays, efforts are made to deny them their human dignity and to do with them whatever one pleases, taking their lives and passing laws preventing anyone from standing in the way of this.[16]

Francis links this abortion mentality to the way elderly are treated."Every elderly person, even if he is ill, or at the end of his days, bears the face of Christ. They cannot be discarded as 'the culture of waste' suggests! They cannot be thrown away!"[17] Francis' concern for the environment is linked to this culture of waste:

> We are experiencing a moment of crisis; we see it in the environment, but mostly we see it in man. The human being is at stake; here is the urgency of human ecology! And the danger is serious because the cause of the problem is not superficial, but profound...The system continues as before. So men and women are sacrificed to the idols of profit and consumption; this is 'scrap culture', the culture of the disposable...So people are discarded, as if they were trash.[18]

Francis links the economy to issues of life, human dignity, and war:

> The world economy will only develop if it allows a dignified way of life for all human beings, from the eldest to the unborn child...for every inhabitant of the earth, even those in extreme social situations or in the remotest places. From this standpoint, it is clear that, for the world's peoples, armed conflicts are always a deliberate negation of international harmony, and create profound divisions and deep wounds which require many years to heal. Wars are a concrete refusal to pursue the great economic and social goals that the international community has set itself. Unfortunately, the many armed conflicts which continue to afflict the world today present us daily with dramatic images of misery, hunger, illness and death.[19]

One billion people suffer from hunger in our world today. Many of them die from it. Francis argues this is a life issue connected to the church's doctrine on ownership of property:

> It is well known that present production is sufficient, and yet millions of persons continue to suffer and die from hunger, and this is a real scandal. We need, then, to find ways by which all may benefit from the fruits of the earth, not only to avoid the widening gap between those who have more and those who must be content with crumbs, but above all because it is a question of justice, equality and respect for every human being. In this regard, I would like to remind everyone of that necessary universal destination of all goods which is one of the fundamental principles of the Church's social teaching.[20]

Francis also has addressed issues of human trafficking, migrants and refugees, prison reform, and capital punishment. Human trafficking involves both some intrinsic evils (forced prostitution) and non-intrinsic but structural evils (forced labor). But the forced prostitution is seen as a kind of labor. Those who would break the link between structural evils and intrinsic evil will never adequately address the intrinsic evil of this reality. Francis notes,

> There are millions of victims of forced labor, victims of human trafficking for the purpose of manual work and of sexual exploitation. This cannot continue. It constitutes a grave violation of the human rights of those victimized and is an offense against their dignity. People of good will, whether or not they profess religious beliefs, must not allow these women, men and children to be treated as objects, to be deceived, raped, often sold and resold for various purposes, and in the end either killed or left devastated in mind and body, only to be finally thrown away or abandoned. It is shameful.[21]

Francis has also condemned capital punishment as inhumane.

It seems quite obvious to me that only a consistent ethic of life does justice to the range of Catholic concerns for solidarity, the common good, economic justice, and respect for human dignity. An exclusive focus on abortion, euthanasia, and gay marriage runs the risk of being seen as mere cultural war and too often overlooks some of the deepest roots of intrinsic evils. Only a consistent ethic of life does justice to the God of mercy—of a call to choose life that Christians espouse.

1   Joseph Cardinal Bernardin, *Consistent Ethic of Life* (New York: Sheed and Ward, 1988), 2.

2   Ibid., 89.

3   Ibid., 10.

4   Ibid., 15. For a good overview of Bernardin's consistent ethic of life cf. Sydney Callahan, "The Consistent Ethic of Life," in *University of Saint Thomas Law Journal*, Vol 2, no. 2 (Spring 2005): 272-293.

5   George Weigel, "The End of the Bernardin Era," *First Things* (February 2011), accessed July 22, 2015, http://www.firstthings.com/article/2011/02/the-end-of-the-bernardin-era.

6   Bishop Robert McElroy, "A Church for the Poor," in *America* (Oct. 21, 2013).

7   Ibid.

8   Ibid.

9   David Gibson, "Cardinal Bernardin's Gift to Pope Francis: The Legacy of the Consistent Ethic of Life" in *Religion News Service* (Oct. 25, 2013), available online in *The Huffington Post* accessed July 22, 2015, http://www.huffingtonpost.com/2013/10/25/cardinal-bernadin-pope-fr_n_4158988.html.

10   Ibid.

11   Pope Francis, "Angelus and Talk to Italy's Pro-Life Movement" (February 1, 2015), accessed July 22, 2015, https://w2.vatican.va/content/francesco/en/angelus/2015/documents/papa-francesco_angelus_20150201.html.

12   Pope Francis, Apostolic Exhortation on the Proclamation of the Gospel in Today's World, *Evangelii Gaudium* (2013), 53. Cited hereafter as EG.

13   Pope Francis, "Message to Muslims Throughout the World at the end of Ramadan" (July 10, 2013), accessed July 22, 2015, https://w2.vatican.va/content/francesco/en/messages/pont-messages/2013/documents/papa-francesco_20130710_musulmani-ramadan.html.

14   The 86 pages of citations from Francis is found on the USCCB's Department of Justice, Peace, and Human Development website: www.USCCB/SDWP.

15   Pope Francis, "General Audience on World Environment Day" (June 5, 2013) accessed July 22, 2015, https://w2.vatican.va/content/francesco/en/audiences/2013/documents/papa-francesco_20130605_udienza-generale.html.

16   EG, 213.

17   Pope Francis, "Address to the International Federation of Catholic Medical Associations" (September 20, 2013), accessed July 22, 2015, http://w2.vatican.va/content/francesco/en/speeches/2013/september/documents/papa-francesco_20130920_associazioni-medici-cattolici.html.

18   Pope Francis, "General Audience on U.N. Environment Day."

19   Pope Francis, "Letter to Vladimir Putin on the Occasion of the G-20 Summit" (September 4, 2013), accessed July 22, 2013, http://w2.vatican.va/content/francesco/en/letters/2013/documents/papa-francesco_20130904_putin-g20.html.

20   Pope Francis, "Message for the World Day of Peace" (December 8, 2013), accessed July 22, 2015, https://w2.vatican.va/content/francesco/en/messages/peace/documents/papa-francesco_20131208_messaggio-xlvii-giornata-mondiale-pace-2014.html.

21 Pope Francis, "Address to New Ambassadors" (December 12, 2013), accessed July 22, http://w2.vatican.va/content/francesco/en/speeches/2013/december/ documents/papa-francesco_20131212_credenziali-nuovi-ambasciatori.pdf.

THE CHURCH AS A FIELD HOSPITAL: THE ECCLESIOLOGY OF POPE FRANCIS

ERIN BRIGHAM

I see clearly that the thing the church needs most today is the ability *to heal wounds and to warm the hearts* of the faithful; *it needs nearness,* proximity. I see the church as a field hospital after battle. It is useless to ask a seriously injured person if he has high cholesterol and about the level of his blood sugars! You have to heal his wounds. Then we can talk about everything else. Heal the wounds, heal the wounds...And you have to start from the ground up.[1]

TO HEAL WOUNDS AND TO WARM HEARTS: POPE FRANCIS ON THE MISSION OF THE CHURCH

In the above quote from a 2013 interview with Antonio Spadaro, S.J., Pope Francis offers a glimpse into his ecclesiology, presenting the church as a field hospital. His chosen image places the church in the midst of human suffering, emphasizing the healing ministry of Jesus

Erin Brigham is the Coordinator of Research for the Joan and Ralph Lane Center for Catholic Studies and Social Thought at the University of San Francisco, where she also teaches in the areas of Catholic theology and ethics. Her published works include: *See, Judge, Act: Catholic Social Teaching and Service Learning* (Anselm Academic, 2013) and *Sustaining the Hope for Unity: Ecumenical Dialogue in a Post-modern World* (Liturgical Press, 2012).

as the foundation for the church's mission. Pope Francis has modeled this understanding of the church in a number of ways, embracing all people—particularly the poor—in the midst of their own battles. Among the examples, during his first year as pope, Francis washed the feet of women and men in a juvenile detention center on Holy Thursday. That year he also visited a community of migrants on the island of Lampedusa and challenged the world to overcome apathy toward their suffering. More recently, he welcomed a group of homeless people on a tour of the Sistine Chapel, reminding all Catholics that their church is a church for the poor. In these situations and more, Francis places himself on the margins of society, in solidarity with those living in poverty, and in doing so, manifests the church as a field hospital.

By instructing ministers to not only heal wounds but also *warm hearts*, Francis emphasizes the importance of leading by authentic witness. Francis has consistently denounced clericalism and has challenged church leaders to model simplicity and humility in their lifestyles. As pope, he has manifested this vision of leadership in a number of ways—opting to live in community instead of the papal apartment and driving a modest vehicle. The pope eschews grand titles, describing himself simply and humbly as a sinner.[2] And when probed about gay priests in the Catholic Church, the pope opts for inclusivity over condemnation in his often quoted reply, "who am I to judge?"[3] Such acts of humility and inclusivity have warmed the hearts of Catholics and non-Catholics alike.

Francis discussed the theological significance of warming hearts in his July 2013 address to the Brazilian bishops. Using the story of the disciples on the road to Emmaus, he emphasizes the importance of being a community who accompanies people on their journey through life, giving particular attention to those who have left the church. He implores the bishops, "I would like all of us to ask ourselves today: are we still a Church capable of warming hearts?"[4] The ministry of warming hearts involves dialogue, meeting people where they are, and walking with them. Instead of condemning the secular culture for pulling people away from the church, he invites self-examination—why have they left and what can church leaders do to serve them?

Francis' speech, directed to the church of Brazil, is also relevant for the United States. Polls have shown a large number of people, particularly those under age 30, choosing not to affiliate with any organized religion. This number has been on the rise over the past decade, with unaffiliated people or "nones" increasing from 15 percent to 20 percent between 2007 and 2012. One theory describing the trend points to the perception among young people that organized religion is too heavily aligned with conservative U.S. politics. In their view, religion is assumed to be narrowly focused on highly politicized social issues such as same-sex marriage and abortion.[5]

In this context, Pope Francis' challenge to prioritize poverty is a heartwarming move that could potentially establish greater credibility for the U.S. Catholic Church. Indeed, the majority of Americans view Francis favorably. And his appeal extends beyond the liberal-conservative political divide, with seven in ten adults expressing a positive view of the pope.[6] One of the reasons the pope is viewed favorably is that he is perceived to embody the core values of Christianity—extending mercy toward the marginalized and demonstrating humility in his words and actions. In a poll conducted by the Pew Research Forum on perceptions of Pope Francis, one respondent summarized this view, "He's going to bring us back to the core values of the church and do things for the people, and not so much the politics or the business of the church."[7] Another young respondent said, "I think what's important is reducing poverty... as opposed to fighting against gay marriage and abortion and contraception...So Pope Francis has done a good job bringing the right things back into focus, and that has certainly changed the way I feel about my church."[8] It is clear that if the Catholic Church is going to warm the hearts of the faithful in the United States, it is going to have to speak to their real concerns. As Francis stated, it needs to address the real wounds before speaking about anything else.

Thomas Reese draws upon Francis' use of the Emmaus story to summarize some key features of the pope's ecclesiology. First,

Francis invites ministers to act not as distant administrators but as pastors—walking with people and meeting them where they are. He emphasizes the importance of witness in sharing the church's message. Pastors should particularly demonstrate the church's mercy through reconciliation and inclusivity. Finally, there is a need for less centralization and greater solidarity and collegiality to highlight the diversity in unity of the Catholic Church. These are among the themes Pope Francis develops in his 2013 Apostolic Exhortation on the Proclamation of the Gospel, *Evangelii Gaudium.*

THE NEED FOR NEARNESS: POPE FRANCIS' ECCLESIOLOGY OF ENCOUNTER

Francis does not set out to develop a comprehensive ecclesiology in *Evangelii Gaudium,* but the document offers insight into his understanding of the church. The pope begins his reflection on the proclamation of the Gospel with a simple invitation, "I invite all Christians, everywhere, at this very moment, to a renewed personal encounter with Jesus Christ, or at least an openness to letting him encounter them; I ask all of you to do this unfailingly each day."[9] This encounter with God's love, for Francis, is the foundation of the church's activity in the world. And Francis has been clear throughout his papacy that if one wants to encounter Christ, they should turn to the poor. Walter Kasper describes the significance of encounter in Francis' understanding of the church, "...we touch upon the deepest—I would say the mystical—dimension of Pope Francis' ecclesiology. He wants to encounter Christ—indeed, to touch Christ—in the poor..."[10]

Francis presents an understanding of the church that reflects the ecclesiology of the Second Vatican Council. By emphasizing the importance of encounter, Francis reinforces the church's solidarity with humanity developed in the Pastoral Constitution on the Church in the Modern World, *Gaudium et Spes.* This document presents the church squarely within human history, taking on "the joys and the hopes, the griefs and the anxieties" of everyone, "especially those who are poor or in any way afflicted."[11] This insight captured in *Gaudium et Spes* follows from the recognition that the church and the world are made up of the same people—historically situated, called to holiness but imperfect on the journey toward God. The pilgrim quality of the church is reinforced by the theological concept of the people of God.

Following the Second Vatican Council's Dogmatic Constitution on the Church, *Lumen Gentium*, which presents the church as the People of God prior to its hierarchical expression, Francis writes, "The Church, as the agent of evangelization, is more than an organic and hierarchical institution; she is first and foremost a people advancing on its pilgrim way towards God."[12] Ecclesiologist Richard Gaillardetz suggests that Francis' preference for the image of the church as the People of God reclaims a central image of Vatican II, which for decades had been overshadowed by an understanding of the church as *communio,* which emphasizes structured communion.[13] And while Francis embraces the church as *communio,* "She is certainly a mystery rooted in the Trinity…,"[14] his emphasis on the People of God allows him to stress the historical nature of the church and prioritize the people who make up the church over its visible structures, "… she exists concretely in history as a people of pilgrims and evangelizers, transcending any institutional expression, however necessary."[15]

The concept of the People of God emphasizes baptism as the primary way to participate in the life of Christ and the ministry of the church. This ecclesiology reinforces the role of the laity in the church and rejects attitudes that elevate the clergy above the rest of the faithful. As Kasper states, "On the basis of his theology of the people of God, Pope Francis is averse to every form of clericalism."[16] Denouncing clericalism, Francis stresses that the ordained ministers should be at the service of the faithful.[17] He also notes that in some cases the laity have not realized their call to participate fully in the life of the church because "excessive clericalism which keeps them away from decision-making."[18]

Francis advocates for greater lay participation in the decision making of the church, giving particular attention to women whose gifts have not been fully recognized.[19] Providing a theological basis for this view, Francis draws upon the concept of the *sensus fidei*—the sense of the faith that allows all the baptized to come to know God.[20] The same Spirit that empowers the laity to discern what is of God also enables the bishops to exercise their teaching role in the church. By recognizing the whole church as recipients of divine truth, this view emphasizes the need for dialogue between the bishops and the faithful.

Francis' understanding of the *sensus fidei* is inseparable from the preferential option for the poor. He writes, "This is why I want a Church which is poor and for the poor. They have much to teach us. Not only do they share in the *sensus fidei*, but in their difficulties they know the suffering Christ. We need to let ourselves be evangelized by them."[21] Liberation theologians speak of this epistemological privilege of the poor, which is foundational in Francis' ecclesiology of encounter. Christ proclaimed the kingdom of God as good news to the poor and powerless. The church therefore should locate itself with those on the margins of society and allow itself to be transformed by them into a church of the poor.

In his words and actions, Francis has challenged the Catholic Church to be the church of the poor. In doing so, he has warmed many hearts—Catholics, non-Catholics, religious, and "nones"—with the joy of the Gospel. In his reflection on the significance of periphery in Pope Francis' ecclesiology, Massimo Faggioli offers an explanation as to why his message has been so appealing. "In the eyes of most Christians, whether Catholic or non-Catholic, an authentic church is a poor church and a church for the poor."[22]

1   Pope Francis in an interview with Antonio Spadaro, S.J., "A Big Heart Open to God," in *America* magazine (September 30th, 2013). Italics mine.

2   Pope Francis, "A Big Heart Open to God."

3   Reported in an interview with Pope Francis on a flight from Brazil to Rome, July 2013. See Rachel Donadio, "On Gay Priests, Pope Francis Asks 'Who am I to Judge?' in *The New York Times* (July 23, 2013), accessed on May 1, 2015, http://www.nytimes.com/2013/07/30/world/europe/pope-francis-gay-priests.html.

4   Address from Pope Francis to the Bishops of Brazil (July 28, 2013), accessed May 1, 2015, https://w2.vatican.va/content/francesco/en/speeches/2013/july/documents/papa-francesco_20130727_gmg-episcopato-brasile.html.

5   Pew Research Center, "Nones on the Rise" (October 2, 2012), accessed April 1, 2015, http://www.pewforum.org/2012/10/09/nones-on-the-rise/.

6   Pew Research Center, "In U.S., Pope's Popularity Continues to Grow" (March 5, 2015), accessed May 1, 2015, http://www.pewforum.org/2015/03/05/in-u-s-popes-popularity-continues-to-grow/.

7   Pew Research Center, "How U.S. Catholics View Pope Francis: In Their Own Words" (March 6, 2014), accessed May 1, 2015, http://www.pewforum.org/2014/03/06/how-catholics-view-pope-francis-in-their-own-words/.

8   Pew Research Center, "How U.S. Catholics View Pope Francis."

9   Pope Francis, Apostolic Exhortation on the Proclamation of the Gospel, *Evangelii Gaudium* (2013), 3. Cited hereafter as EG.

10 Walter Kasper, "Open House: How Pope Francis Sees the Church," in *Commonweal Magazine* (March 13, 2015).

11 Second Vatican Council, Pastoral Constitution on the Church in the Modern World, *Gaudium et Spes* (1965), 1. Cited hereafter as GS.

12 EG, 111.

13 Richard Gaillardetz, "The Francis Moment: A New Kairos for Catholic Ecclesiology," The Presidential address for the Catholic Theological Society of America 2014, in *CTSA Proceedings* 69 (2014).

14 EG, 111.

15 Ibid.

16 Kasper, "Open House."

17 EG, 102.

18 Ibid.

19 Pope Francis, "A Big Heart Open To God."

20 EG, 119.

21 Ibid., 189.

22 Massimo Faggioli, "Vatican II and the Church of the Margins" in *Theological Studies* Vol 74 (2013), 812.

INTRINSIC EVIL: A GUIDE FOR THE PERPLEXED

WILLIAM O'NEILL, S.J.

"Intrinsic evil"—these are words to conjure with. Opposing intrinsically evil acts, it would seem, trumps all other moral concerns in magisterial teaching. Intrinsic evils, like artificial contraception or abortion, are "nonnegotiable" in public policy; while prudential opposition to poverty or violence remains "optional." But there are other trump cards in morality's deck, and not all of them involve intrinsic evil. What do we mean, then, when we say an act is intrinsically evil? Does calling an act "intrinsically evil" suffice to determine its relative gravity? And what are the implications of laws, policies, or practices permitting intrinsic evil in religiously pluralist polities like our own? Let us briefly consider each question.

INTERPRETING INTRINSIC EVIL

The greatest treason, says T. S. Eliot, is to do the right deed for the wrong reason. But there is treason too in doing the wrong deed for the right reason. For Aristotle and his medieval interpreter, St. Thomas Aquinas, we act morally when we do the right deed, for

William O'Neill, S.J. is Associate Professor of Social Ethics at the Jesuit School of Theology. His writings address questions of human rights, ethics and hermeneutical theory, social reconciliation and conflict resolution, and refugee policy. He has worked with refugees in Tanzania and Malawi and has done research on human rights in South Africa and Rwanda. He currently serves on the board of the Society of Christian Ethics and the journal *Theological Studies*.

the right reasons, under the right circumstances. And so it is that the rich casuistic tradition of Roman Catholic moral theology distinguishes three fonts of moral action: the object, or what defines the action as such; the reasons that motivate us, i.e., our intention; and the circumstances and consequences we foresee. Typically, any moral assessment of what we do entails both backward-looking considerations of intention and forward-looking considerations of circumstances, including consequences.

Yet circumstances, consequences, and intentions do not alone determine the morality of action. Certain acts are rendered morally impermissible by their "object." As St. Paul admonishes us, we can never do what is morally evil to achieve good (Rom. 3:8). So too, for Aquinas, "An evil action cannot be justified by reference to a good intention."[1] In the words of the *Catechism*, "There are acts which, in and of themselves, independently of circumstances and intentions, are always gravely illicit by reason of their object; such as blasphemy and perjury, murder and adultery."[2] Such actions are "intrinsically evil" (*intrinsece malum*), says John Paul II in his encyclical *Veritatis splendor*, if they are "*per se* and in themselves, independently of circumstances… always seriously wrong by virtue of their object."[3] The "*object of the choice*" can, then, "by itself vitiate an act in its entirety."[4] Intrinsically evil acts specify the evil that must be avoided if, as the natural law prescribes, "good is to be done." No further appeal to intentions, circumstances, or consequences ever suffices to justify them. Indeed, John Paul II is sharply critical of revisionist moral theologians who appeal to proportionate reason in evaluating the "object as source of morality."[5] But how do we know an act is intrinsically evil? Again we look to Aquinas, who tells us that prudence (*prudentia*) orders all actions as means (instrumental or constitutive) to human flourishing. And it is prudence that reveals certain means as morally impermissible, e.g., "blasphemy and perjury, murder and adultery. One may not do evil so that good may result from it."[6] Here, the tradition appeals to what we might call a "perfectionist teleology"—a method of moral reasoning that determines the rightness or wrongness of an action by assessing it in light of its natural "end" or "goal" (*telos*, in Greek).

Only those actions compatible with human perfection (for Aristotle and Aquinas, a fully virtuous life) are morally justified. Conversely, actions "incapable of being ordered to God" are, by their nature or object, immoral.[7] Blasphemy betrays the covenantal fidelity at the heart of biblical justice; perjury undermines the juridical institution of truth-telling; acts fittingly described as "murder" are per definition unjust, and adultery belies the natural moral ends of matrimony. Whether an act necessarily falls under the fitting description is sometimes subject to dispute, e.g., is a given act of homicide rightly described as murder? But once so described, an act is never morally permissible.

Variations on the theme extend the category of intrinsic evil to other acts. Thus the magisterium teaches that recourse to artificial contraception, masturbation, and same-sex genital relations are, by their nature, intrinsically evil.[8] The gravamen of the argument in these cases turns less on human flourishing or perfection than on the perfection of the sexual act. In church teaching, the individual act of sexual intercourse, independently of circumstances or intention, is naturally ordered to procreation. Consequentially, any artificial interference with the act (contraception) or non-procreative use (masturbation or same-sex genital relations) is viewed as "*contra naturam*" (against nature) and hence, forbidden.

And still, a third variation is wrung in modern magisterial teaching. "The Second Vatican Council itself," says John Paul II, "in discussing the respect due to the human person, gives a number of examples of such acts," e.g., "any kind of homicide, genocide, abortion, euthanasia and voluntary suicide...mutilation, physical and mental torture and attempts to coerce the spirit...subhuman living conditions, arbitrary imprisonment, deportation, slavery, prostitution and trafficking in women and children; degrading conditions of work..."[9] In accordance with the Conciliar tenor of Catholic social teaching, the church appeals to the fundamental respect owed moral persons in virtue of their innate dignity (their creation in the *imago dei*) and derivative human rights. The argument, that is, turns less on a particular interpretation of human perfection about which religiously pluralist societies differ, much less on the perfection of individual acts, than on respect for human dignity and equal human rights. We see here an interpretative shift that enlarges the scope of intrinsically evil acts. Only in *Veritatis splendor* is slavery, heretofore seen as consistent with natural law, classified as intrinsically evil.

The turn to dignity and equal human rights likewise qualifies *how* we understand intrinsic evil. For centuries, interest-bearing loans were condemned as intrinsically evil since monetary transactions, it was believed, could not "naturally" be reproductive. Today, by contrast, the church condemns usury, not as interest-taking per se, but as excessive or exorbitant interest that denies the respect due moral persons. Actions fittingly described as usurious are never permissible. But their impermissibility rests not in the "nature" of interest-taking, but on a consequentially sensitive assessment of what counts as excessive or exorbitant interest.

INTRINSIC EVIL AND RELATIVE MORAL GRAVITY

That an act is morally impermissible does not immediately establish the degree of moral gravity. Lying, for instance (so Augustine believed), is never permissible, but certainly not all instances of lying are equally grave. Not all equally imperil human flourishing. So, too, several of the practices John Paul describes as intrinsically evil admit of degree, e.g., attempts to coerce the spirit, subhuman living conditions, degrading conditions of work, etc. But certain actions, behavior, and practices, e.g., slavery or genocide, so clearly and systematically violate human dignity and basic human rights, that we condemn them as gravely evil *tout court*. No appeal to collective ends such as natural security or beneficent consequences can ever justify such "barbarous acts which have outraged the conscience" of humanity.[10]

Certain actions, then, are impermissible simply because they are gravely evil. Abortion, for instance, is forbidden because it denies the dignity and rights of those most vulnerable. Yet not all intrinsically evil acts are equally grave. Neither masturbation nor artificial contraception perspicuously offend against human dignity or persons' basic rights (as we noted above, describing them as intrinsically evil rests on different grounds—the metaphysical finality of the act of intercourse). It is possible, of course, to subsume such act-centered condemnation under the modern rubrics of dignity and rights; but further argumentation is needed, especially in a religiously pluralist polity.

And if not all intrinsically evil actions, behavior, or practices are equally grave, so not all gravely evil actions, behavior, and practices are intrinsically evil. As Bishop McElroy has persuasively argued, inequitable practices culminating in endemic poverty are no less an affront to the dignity of the most vulnerable than abortion.[11] Abortion is gravely wrong for precisely the same reason willfully abandoning women to sexual assault and death on our southwest deserts is wrong: both are grave offenses against "the respect due to the human person," though the former act is gravely wrong in virtue of its object and the latter in virtue of its intention and consequences.

THE POLITICS OF INTRINSIC EVIL

If we err in failing to distinguish intrinsic and grave evil; so too we err in conflating personal and social choice. If I believe that an action is rightly described as intrinsically evil, in no circumstances can *I* perform it. I cannot do what I regard as morally evil, even in lesser matters, to achieve good. Yet personal conscience is not "writ large" on the body politic. As Aquinas recognized, not all wrongful actions are necessarily fit subjects of legislative proscription—not all fall under the rubrics of justice. So, too, a permissive law may be morally flawed; but voting for it does not represent complicity in intrinsic evil if it limits the harm done. A law permitting intrinsic evil in a democratic polity is not, for that reason, itself intrinsically evil.

Rather, wise politics asks which feasible policy *best* protects the rights of the most vulnerable. John Paul II himself appeals to such prudential logic in *Evangelium Vitae*, arguing that one "could licitly support proposals aimed at limiting the harm done by such a law and at lessening its negative consequences …This does not in fact represent an illicit cooperation with an unjust law, but rather a legitimate and proper attempt to limit its evil aspects."[12] Now, John Paul II is not saying that abortion is permissible for proportionate reasons. The question, rather, is how best to "limit the evil aspects" of prevailing policies, laws, or practices. For in this case, the lesser evil *is* the greater good. As John Paul reminds us, such prudential reasoning, legitimately and properly, pertains to abortion policy. Prudence favors every reasonable legal measure "limiting the harm done"—to both fetus *and* vulnerable mother. And among these, surely, is securing the social-economic rights, including health care, of women whose poverty and vulnerability remain a leading cause of abortion.

Prudence, after all, must determine whether we vote for a permissive law, e.g., in the case of abortion; whether we seek a religious exemption, e.g., in the case of contraception; or whether we seek a repeal of law deemed unjust, e.g., Jim Crow laws. Indeed, as we saw above, in the Thomistic tradition, it is prudence that reveals certain actions as intrinsically evil; just as prudence determines the comparative gravity of evil actions and the appropriate political response. There is no simple recipe for the moral life dispensing us from exercising practical wisdom or prudence. Neither can we succumb to a moral myopia that opposes a "nonnegotiable" morality of intrinsically evil actions (often restricted to sexual matters) to an "optional" morality of prudence, e.g., poverty.

CONCLUSIONS

Intrinsic evil, we may conclude, is a useful but limited term of art in moral casuistry: Useful, inasmuch as the interpretation of intrinsically evil acts reflects our cumulative moral learning (certain actions, behavior, or practices, we have come to see, are never permissible, e.g., slavery, racism, rape, or abortion). But limited, inasmuch as not all intrinsically evil acts are equally grave (lying or masturbation cannot be equated with slavery, racism, rape, or abortion). And not all morally grave actions, behavior, or practices, e.g., systemic deprivation culminating in poverty, are necessarily intrinsically evil. Nor, as we saw, does the mere determination of intrinsic evil decide policy or legislative remedy. Conscience, of course, does not make casuists of us all. But as Aquinas realized long ago, moral virtue turns on practical wisdom or prudence. In a fallen world of fallible agents, only the wisdom of serpents preserves the innocence of doves.

1   Thomas Aquinas, *Collationes in decem praeceptis*, 6.

2   *Catechism of the Catholic Church* (1993), 1756.

3   Pope John Paul II, Encyclical Regarding Certain Fundamental Questions of the Church's Moral Teaching, *Veritatis Splendor* (1993), 80; cited hereafter as VS, cf. John Paul II, Apostolic Exhortation on Reconciliation and Penance in the Mission of the Church Today, *Reconcilatio et Paenitentia* (1984), 17.

4   *Catechism*, 1755.

5   VS, 82.

6   *Catechism*, 1756.

7   VS, 80.

8   Significantly, the Catechism teaches that a same-sex *orientation* is not, per se, intrinsically evil, *Catechism*, 2358.

9   VS, 80.

10 United Nations, *Universal Declaration of Human Rights* (1948), Preamble.

11 Robert McElroy, "A Church for the Poor," in *America* magazine (October 21, 2013).

12 John Paul II, Encyclical on the Value and Inviolability of Human Life, *Evangelium Vitae* (1995), 73.

CONFRONTING THE "ECONOMY OF EXCLUSION" FROM THE GROUND UP

JOHN BAUMANN, S.J.

Of all the beautiful and provocative imagery that Pope Francis has painted with his words and deeds over the last two years, perhaps my favorite is that of the church as a field hospital in the midst of battle. In April 2015, I joined nearly 300 Catholic clergy and grassroots lay leaders from across the PICO (People Improving Communities through Organizing) National Network and Jesuit Conference to hear my friend and colleague in the ministry, Honduran Cardinal Oscar Rodriguez Maradiaga, share with us his same love for this metaphor. It was Cardinal Rodriguez who first invited PICO into Central America.

PICO is an international network of faith-based community organizations working to create innovative solutions to problems facing urban, suburban, and rural communities. Since 1972, PICO has successfully worked to increase access to health care, improve

John Baumann, S.J. is PICO founder and Director of Special Projects. Nationally, PICO serves a network of 55 congregation, faith-based community organizations in over 250 cities in 20 states. Internationally, PICO is developing organizations in El Salvador, Guatemala, Rwanda in East Africa, and Haiti. PICO assists in the building of community organizations with the power to improve the quality of life of families and neighborhoods through leadership training seminars; the recruitment and development of professional community organizers; on-going consultation; and technical assistance. PICO also serves as a vehicle for state-wide and national organizing.

public schools, make neighborhoods safer, build affordable housing, redevelop communities, and revitalize democracy. PICO helps engage ordinary people in public life, building a strong legacy of leadership in thousands of local communities across America, Central America, Haiti, and Rwanda.

In our meeting, Cardinal Rodriguez, who chairs the Council of Cardinals advising Pope Francis, listened to a series of testimonies from PICO grassroots leaders. These included Rev. Juard Barnes, an African-American man suffering from a criminal justice system that unfairly targets and harms people of color; Antonio Campos, an undocumented immigrant who taught college in Mexico but, after 20 years in the United States, continues to scrub toilets for a living; Serena Santos, who after seven years working for a multi-billion dollar airline continues to make minimum wage and get no sick time; and Mary Vitcenda, a middle-class woman who shared the pain and shame she experienced after losing her job and home during the economic downturn.

After listening to these testimonies, Cardinal Rodriguez said this:

> In the Joy of the Gospel, the Pope says that explicitly I have a dream. I dream of a different Church that can go especially as a field hospital–I love that image because what I heard from these brothers and sisters this morning are the wounds of an unjust society, that an unjust system has caused them. This must not continue. But the Church has to be near those who suffer. That's why he was using this image of a field hospital. During a war, when you have people that are wounded, you cannot stay in the big hospital and say 'come, come you're mostly welcome.' No, you need to go there in the middle of them to heal immediately the wounds. This is our project. This is our dream. This is why PICO exists.

A little over two years into Francis' papacy, Catholics all over the globe are beginning to discern how they can move beyond just watching and applauding the tremendous "dream" that Pope Francis is setting out for the church, but actually *participate* in his papacy and the enactment of his vision of a "field hospital" church. That was the purpose of our 300-person gathering with Cardinal Rodriguez. PICO and the Jesuit Conference of United States and Canada together have launched an initiative we are calling the "Year of Encounter: Confronting the Economy of Exclusion." This is a year-long faith formation and social action program timed around the build-up to and aftermath of Pope Francis' visit to the United States in the fall of 2015. This initiative seeks to take Pope Francis' vision of a "field hospital" church and manifest it more broadly across the 500 parishes that participate in PICO, as well as hundreds of other parishes moved by Pope Francis and seeking to take action.

This initiative is also in direct response to the Francis' persistent call to build a "culture of encounter" and "culture of solidarity," where Catholics "go forth" and seek out Christ in everyone, and especially the poor and others whom society has pushed to the margins. By "encounter," Francis calls us to allow this experience to transform our own hearts and minds, to see the world anew from their vantage point. And finally, lest one forget Francis' stinging critique of "the economy of exclusion and inequality" and consistent call to Catholics to be involved in political life, he is demanding that people act together to confront the forces of idolatry that put wealth, power, or status above God's people and hold politicians accountable to gospel values.

As I've been reading and learning more about Pope Francis, formerly Cardinal Jorge Bergoglio, I am struck by just how much this notion of "encounter," manifested in countless personal relationships with poor and excluded people in Argentina, deeply formed his perspectives and vision of a field hospital church. As a Jesuit provincial in the 1970s, he sent Jesuit students out on weekend missions in poor neighborhoods to root them in the reality of "God's holy faithful people." He eventually led the Jesuits in building a vibrant new parish spanning multiple poor barrios that included a working farm to employ and feed people, schools, and medical clinics.

As Austen Ivereigh writes in *The Great Reformer*, this parish,

> ...embodied Bergoglio's vision of a radical apostolate geared to the peripheries. Rather than put up a sign with Mass times outside the church and wait for people to come, he sectioned the area off into zones, assigned dozens of Jesuit students to each one, and sent them out through dusty or muddy streets to visit households.[1]

Never one to be above doing himself what he expected of others, Bergoglio worked side by side with neighborhood residents and the Jesuit students in doing menial farm tasks.

Years later, during his installation as auxiliary bishop of Buenos Aires, he stood out from the other bishops being ordained that day because of the many people who greeted and congratulated him: the poor people with whom he had built relationships over the years. As a bishop, Bergoglio spent much of his time attending to people in poor neighborhoods in Buenos Aires, and deploying priests to work in these barrios. As Ivereigh notes in his book, in one particular barrio, one-half of the residents—roughly 25,000 people!—are said to have met him. And this was just in one barrio.

In an article Fr. Bergoglio penned in 1980 on apostolic action, he warned against the approach of the "enlightened classes" who were "for the people, but never with the people." Instead, he wrote that apostolic action must start from direct contact with the poor. "The true possibilities of justice in the world," he wrote in another document, could only be realized by sharing in the lives of the poor.[2] PICO responds to this challenge by meeting the people where they are through one-to-one visits and house meetings, and inviting them to bring their stories into action that confronts systems of exclusion.

I would argue that the Holy Father's immense popularity worldwide is in large part due to his authentic, unwavering commitment to "smelling like his sheep." He acts and speaks as someone who knows—and has never lost touch with—the experiences and pain of real people. The poor and excluded are not theoretical concepts for him; they are, like Christ, flesh and blood beings with aspirations and challenges that he can understand and articulate. Or as Cardinal Rodriguez said to us in April,

> One of the problems of this system that we are living in is that it considers poverty only as figures, numbers. For us it's very different. For us poverty is concrete faces, concrete persons, with names and families, with their age and with their environment where they grew up, where they work, where they raise their families. This is the poverty we have to overcome … and the first step is to be organized.

Ordinary people can sense Francis' authenticity and deep respect for them. Because he understands their lived experiences, he can articulate the material and spiritual pain they face like few others can. And he is unafraid to be a "moral conscience" for the world at a time when such a conscience is sorely needed, denouncing the idolatrous forces that have displaced people from the center of our economy and society.

With the United States preparing for Pope Francis' first visit to our country this fall, we are more than ever in need of voices rooted deeply in relationship with the poor and excluded that can help us rediscover our moral conscience. The poorest 47 percent of Americans today own *zero* wealth (i.e., their debt exceeds their assets). Meanwhile, the 400 wealthiest Americans together own more wealth than the bottom 80 million families (62 percent of America).[3] Here in the richest nation on earth, where corporate profits reached record levels in the last few years, one in five children—and more than one in three children of color—live in poverty.[4] Research shows that babies born to poor moms in the U.S. are twice as likely to die in their first year than babies born to wealthier moms.[5] This is a matter of life and death.

The United States incarcerates more people than any other country on the planet. Over the past 30 years, the prison population has grown 500 percent. There are more people locked up in the U.S. than in China.[6] Black males are incarcerated at a staggeringly disproportionate rate—one in every three black males born today can expect to go to prison at some point in his life, compared with one in every 17 white males.[7]

The country's eagerness to incarcerate people extends to immigrant families as well. The United States now operates family detention centers holding thousands of immigrant mothers and their young children awaiting immigration hearings. The conditions in these centers are dismal, and the mental and spiritual impacts of imprisoning *children* are devastating.[8] Meanwhile, 11 million undocumented immigrants, who came to the U.S. in search of a better life for their families, instead live every day in fear that their families will be torn apart by deportation.

While these miseries unfold and inflict so much harm on so many Americans, our elected officials who are in a position to make policy aimed at reducing this suffering are more distant than ever from the people they supposedly represent. The median net worth for federal lawmakers was just over $1 million in 2013, or 18 times the wealth of the typical American household.[9] New research shows that politicians are more likely to align with the policy preferences of a tiny sliver of the wealthy than they are with the preferences of the vast numbers of average Americans.[10] More and more in our political discourse, people are being talked *to*, and talked *about*, but not talked *with*.

Amid our hyper-partisan, gridlocked political culture today, we need leaders from the Catholic Church and other religious traditions to make this same call on our politicians—to ignite a "culture of encounter" that, emerging out of the stories of people like Juard Barnes, Serena Santos, and Antonio Campos, has the potential for transformation.

In a lecture at the Universidad del Salvador in 1989, Fr. Bergoglio argued that Argentina had become highly politicized, but had forgotten what politics was for—which, in his view, is to harmonize different interests with the goal of improving the lives of people and to work toward the common good. As Cardinal in Buenos Aires in the early 2000s, Bergoglio, under the banner "culture of encounter," called clearly to politicians across the spectrum to renounce their individual and partisan interests and hear the call of the people.

Today, Pope Francis writes in *The Joy of the Gospel* (*Evangelii Gaudium*) "I beg the Lord to grant us more politicians who are genuinely disturbed by the lives of the poor."[11] At PICO, we believe that, in line with Francis' teaching, our political leaders will only become "disturbed by the lives of the poor" by once again being exposed to the poor and excluded themselves. In other words, the field hospital also needs to be brought to the steps of state capitals across the country and the halls of Congress in Washington, D.C.

That is why PICO and the Jesuits, in the buildup to Pope Francis'

September visit (which perhaps not coincidentally comes just as the Presidential primary season heats up), is launching the "Year of Encounter" effort. We want both to engage thousands of Catholics nationwide around Pope Francis' vision, and we hope to encourage "public encounters" that bring the pain and suffering affecting so many American families directly to the people who want our votes and who should see their missions as helping mitigate that suffering.

In this year of encounter, PICO invites all people of faith to do two things. First, read Pope Francis' *Evangelii Gaudium* and discuss it with family, friends, and fellow congregants. Learn and be inspired. Second, act on what you have read—leave your comfort zone and encounter those who live at the margins of our society. These are people who find themselves excluded from the mainstream by economic, immigration, and criminal justice systems that are too often unfair and unresponsive. As the Gospel reminds us, in encountering people like Rev. Juard Barnes, Antonio Campos, Serena Santos, and Mary Vitcenda, we will encounter Christ. Join them in solidarity as they fight for inclusion and justice. As Pope Francis fully understands, no situation is set in stone. Transformation can happen. It can happen again and again. And it starts with encounter.

1   Austen Ivereigh, *The Great Reformer: Francis and the Making of a Radical Pope* (New York: MacMillan/ Henry Holt, 2014), 180-181.

2   Jorge Bergoglio, "El Reino de Cristo," in *Meditaciones para Religiosos* (Barcelona: Ediciones Diego De Torres, 1982).

3   Inequality for All, accessed July 23, 2015, http://www.inequalityforall.com/fact-3/.

4   Children's Defense Fund, "The State of America's Children 2014" accessed July 23, 2015, http://www.childrensdefense.org/library/state-of-americas-children/documents/2014-.

5   SOAC_overview.pdf.

6   Christopher Ingraham, "Our Infant Mortality Rate is a National Embarrassment," in the Washington Post Wonkblog (September 29, 2014), accessed July 23, 2015, http://www.washingtonpost.com/blogs/wonkblog/

wp/2014/09/29/our-infant-mortality-rate-is-a-national-embarrassment/.

7   The Sentencing Project, "Incarceration," accessed July 23, 2015, http://www.sentencingproject.org/template/page.cfm?id=107.

8   The Sentencing Project, "Report of the Sentencing Project to the United Nations Regarding Racial Disparities in the United States Criminal Justice System" (August 2013), accessed July 23, 2015, http://sentencingproject.org/doc/publications/rd_ICCPR%20Race%20and%20Justice%20Shadow%20Report.pdf.

9   Wil Hylton, "The Shame of America's Family Detention Camps" in *New York Times Magazine* (February 4, 2015), accessed July 23, 2015, http://www.nytimes.com/2015/02/08/magazine/the-shame-of-americas-family-detention-camps.html.

10   CNN Money, "Congress is Getting Richer" (January 12, 2015) accessed July 23, 2015, http://money.cnn.com/2015/01/12/news/economy/congress-wealth/.

11   Noam Scheiber, "2016 Hopefuls and Wealthy are Aligned with Inequality," in *The New York Times* (March 29, 2015), accessed July 29, 2015, http://www.nytimes.com/2015/03/30/business/candidates-and-wealthy-are-aligned-on-inequality.html?ref=politics.

12   Pope Francis, Apostolic Exhortation on the Proclamation of the Gospel in Today's World, *Evangelii Gaudium* (2013), 175. Cited hereafter as EG.

SOLIDARITY AND COMMUNITY ORGANIZING

Joseph Fleming

For those working in the field of faith-based community organizing, the words and actions of Pope Francis for the people pushed to the margins of our society are deeply inspiring. It is exciting and refreshing to experience the pope's clear articulation of the rich tradition of Catholic Social Teaching, announcing the Good News and denouncing systems and structures that exclude some to benefit others.

In *The Joy of the Gospel*, Pope Francis lays out a framework for evangelization that revolves around three compelling core themes: exclusion, encounter, and solidarity.

When he speaks of "an economy of exclusion," Pope Francis describes the effect of an unbridled market economy that devalues the humanity of all, especially those viewed as "unproductive":

> Human beings are themselves considered consumer goods to be used and then discarded. We have created a "throw away" culture which is now spreading. It is no longer simply about exploitation and oppression, but something new. Exclusion ultimately has to do with what it means to be a part of the society in which we live; those excluded are no longer society's underside or its fringes or its disenfranchised—they are no

Joseph Fleming is the Director of Faith in New Jersey, and has organized with faith communities in the Garden State for 25 years with the PICO National Network. A lifelong Catholic, he also leads PICO's work to deepen Catholic engagement in faith-based community organizing across the United States.

longer even a part of it. The excluded are not the "exploited" but the outcast, the "leftovers."[1]

In several cities of New Jersey, where I have organized with faith communities for many years, we can see what it looks like when a community has been deemed as the "outcast" or "leftovers." While many residents demonstrate tremendous resiliency in the face of pervasive poverty, violence, and limited opportunity, those painful economic and social conditions exact a high price on family and community life. In this context, a five-minute drive will take one from a neighborhood of deep poverty to a thriving suburban community that feels light years away.

The economic and political actors in the state—along with the majority of voters—have developed a kind of moral blind spot that allows, or causes, them to not "see" the Camdens and Newarks in our midst. They appear to have made a determination that people who live in these cities are less worthy, largely expendable, and outside their "circle of concern." Candidates for statewide public office rarely even mention growing poverty and income inequality in New Jersey, let alone respond to the need to marshal resources to respond.

This assessment leaves out any analysis of the economic and social systems that have disinvested from our cities over the past 40 years as the demographics of our cities have changed. Of course, race plays a large role in this equation, in both the disinvestment and lack of empathy. Cities like Camden and Newark, largely black and brown and poor, are viewed as less deserving of compassion and support by many suburban white voters because of racial stereotyping and scapegoating. Add to that New Jersey's version of the anti-tax, small-government movements seen nationally and the aforementioned cities become a "problem" to be contained and managed, rather than a moral crisis for the society as a whole. Pope Francis speaks to this:

> Almost without being aware of it, we end up being incapable of feeling compassion at the outcry of the poor, weeping for other people's pain, and feeling a need to help them, as though all this were someone else's responsibility and not our own.[2]

The antidote to exclusion and isolation is "encounter," and in many of his homilies, Pope Francis urges us to create a "culture of encounter." With that phrase, he appears to be promoting outreach to others, dialogue across the usual dividing lines, and a priority for engaging people "at the peripheries"—those marginalized and excluded by society. He famously wrote: "I prefer a Church which is bruised, hurting and dirty because it has been out on the streets, rather than a Church which is unhealthy from being confined and from clinging to its own security."[3] Elsewhere he noted, "Before all else, the Gospel invites us to respond to the God of love who saves us, to see God in others and to go forth from ourselves to seek the good of others."[4]

Pope Francis adds an interesting twist to the notion of encounter by modeling it in different ways at different times. We have all read stories about him picking up the telephone or scheduling a private meeting with someone who has reached out to him for prayer, comfort, or support. These are one-to-one, personal encounters. But we have also seen him conduct very public encounters, sometimes with large groups of people affected by a systemic injustice. An example is his visit to the African migrant community on the Sicilian island of Lampedusa in 2013, when he chose to meet with a group of immigrants in full view of many officials and a large contingent of media. Francis listened to the immigrants' desperate stories of why they left their home countries, the hardship they endured in crossing the Mediterranean, and their mistreatment by the Italian government—and by doing it publicly, he bore witness to the injustice and created moral pressure on political leaders in the region to respond to the crisis.

The parallel to the culture of encounter in the field of faith-based community organizing is our belief in the transforming power of relationships. By purposefully entering into dialogue with one another—by sharing the key experiences, values, and hopes that shape who we are—we can and do bridge differences and develop the trust that makes it possible to address common concerns together. When that is done broadly and deeply, the resulting relationships create the community and cohesion necessary to organize for structural changes that address economic and social exclusion. The investment in relationships channels power in a focused way to bring about changes within the systems that exclude those of us seen as less "worthy"—our economy, our immigration system, and our criminal justice system, among others.

The third element of Pope Francis' framework for evangelization is solidarity. He states:

> The word 'solidarity' is a little worn and at times poorly understood, but it refers to something more than a few sporadic acts of generosity. It presumes the creation of a new mindset which thinks in terms of community and the priority of the life of all over the appropriation of goods by a few.[5]

At times, I have felt some of the ambivalence toward the word "solidarity" to which Pope Francis alludes. Among suburban, middle-class Catholics I have heard it expressed at times as a kind of *noblesse oblige*, a duty to help the less fortunate—"the less fortunate" being, to them, less capable, and therefore needing the help of suburbanites to make any headway. Lacking any foundation in relationship, or real curiosity about other people and their experiences and gifts, the interaction becomes more of a transaction: "we'll supply the expertise, solve the problem, and move along." It is a version of solidarity that gets told from the perspective of privilege.

I would hasten to add here that the understanding of solidarity that is described above does not reflect the richness of the word within Catholic Social Teaching—a deep faith commitment, activated by "encountering" our brothers and sisters and seeing God's image within them, compels us to widen our "circle of concern" to include everyone. And if any one of my brothers and sisters is excluded or diminished, then I am diminished. And if I benefit in some way from systems that exclude others, then I am complicit in that injustice and am morally responsible to work to undo it.

In his speech to the World Meeting of Popular Movements last year, Pope Francis highlighted another essential aspect of solidarity, by telling the story from the vantage point of the oppressed:

> ...the poor will no longer wait; they want to be protagonists; they organize themselves, study, work, claim and, above all, practice that very special solidarity that exists among those who suffer, among the poor, whom our civilization seems to have forgotten...[6]

In this expression of solidarity, Francis recognizes the dignity and capacity of poor and excluded people. They work together to build community and to organize for structural change—they are more than mere "victims" or "objects," but rather subjects who can make history themselves.

Through these words and his acts of "public encounter," Pope Francis is helping us understand that solidarity has two dimensions. To overcome the evil of exclusion in our world, people who are excluded must *stand up* (by organizing, confronting the injustice they experience, and demanding structural change); and others, who do not experience deep exclusion, must *stand with* (by bearing witness to the injustice, joining in demanding change, being willing to forgo the privileges they enjoy, and adding moral and political support to the cause). And, ultimately, we must all take a stand *together*. The culture of encounter makes this kind of deep solidarity possible.

I'll share a simple organizing story that illustrates what solidarity expressed in these multiple ways can look like. I worked a number of years ago with a city parish located in a mostly low-income, black and Latino neighborhood. The church members were mostly white suburbanites who came in each Sunday to worship, but there were also a few parishioners from the neighborhood.

The parish had developed an impressive array of direct services over the years to meet the needs of its neighbors: affordable housing, health services, a clothing store and food pantry, a parish school that provided scholarships to neighborhood children, holiday baskets, and more. The parish was largely viewed with resentment by its neighbors, however, because they had no indication that the pastor and parishioners saw people as more than clients in need of their services. So, they felt disrespected and shamed. Parish staff and church members were puzzled by the lack of appreciation and dismissed the underlying tensions. We might analyze this situation, using Pope Francis' lexicon, as a situation of exclusion in which there was no action of encounter on the part of the parish.

A small team of parishioners gathered one Saturday morning—suburbanites and neighborhood residents—to reflect on the tension and to discern whether they could take any steps to get into a more authentic relationship with the community around the church. Their first movement was to communicate with one another—an initial encounter that led them to develop a plan to do outreach to the broader community over a period of several months. They headed out in pairs to door-knock, one suburban and one neighborhood parishioner in each pairing, and they asked people to talk with them about what it was like to live in their community: What were the positive aspects? What were the things they would want to change, and why?

They then organized a community dinner, at which a larger group of suburban parishioners had one-to-one conversations with a larger group of neighborhood residents about the parish and community. Out of those conversations, a shared concern emerged about a facility in the neighborhood that was generating a significant amount of air pollution. The poor air-quality, in turn, was linked to an increase in asthma among children in the neighborhood.

A growing parish organizing team, with new suburban and neighborhood residents recruited from the community dinner, held meetings with city, county, and state officials to understand the environmental regulations to which the facility was subject. They also met with the owner of the facility. Weeks later, they organized a public meeting—a "public encounter"—to confront the owner and demand that the situation be resolved. Residents publicly shared their testimonies about the negative impact on their health and property values, and suburban parishioners stood with them to call on state officials to hold the owner accountable. Significant media coverage of the meeting helped to increase pressure to resolve the problem. In the end, the owner made commitments to remediate the problem, which he went on to fulfill.

What left the deepest impression on me from that evening was the shared leadership and ownership of the event—a joint leadership team from the neighborhood and parish led the meeting and the 200 people who turned out were almost exactly a 50/50 split between the two communities. While it did not resolve all of the tensions between the two communities, at least for those most involved, it was an experience of deep solidarity that was rooted in relationship, in a budding "culture of encounter" within that parish. Pope Francis is providing new language and new inspiration to understand and replicate the experience.

1   Pope Francis, Apostolic Exhortation on the Proclamation of the Gospel in Today's World, *Evangelii Gaudium* (2013), 53.

2   Ibid., 54.

3   Ibid., 49.

4   Ibid., 39.

5   Ibid., 188.

6   Pope Francis, "Address to Popular Movements," in *Zenit* (October 29, 2014), accessed July 29, 2015, http://www.zenit.org/en/articles/pope-s-address-to-popular-movements.

LATINO IMMIGRATION, FAITH, AND COMMUNITY ORGANIZING: THE SAN FRANCISCO EXPERIENCE

Adriana Guzmán, Lorena Melgarejo, Luis Enrique Bazán

Transforming the existing Catholic political conversation in the United States is a fundamental component to enhance the work with Catholic Latino immigrants in San Francisco. We are community organizers who have worked extensively with Latino immigrant communities in San Francisco and the Bay Area.

Luis Enrique Bazán works at the University of San Francisco, directing the immersion programs and teaching ethics at the St. Ignatius Institute. He has been engaged with community-based organizations for 25 years in Peru, and since 2002 in San Francisco.

Adriana Guzman joined the San Francisco Organizing Project/Peninsula Interfaith Action (SFOP/PIA) as an organizer who started as a volunteer leader during PICO's Campaign for Citizenship in 2013. As a volunteer, she led several campaigns to stop immigrants from being deported and has done extensive outreach in immigrant congregations throughout San Francisco and San Mateo Counties. Adriana is currently leading SFOP/PIA's effort to provide information about the new drivers' license and deferred action for children and parents to all immigrant congregations on the SF Peninsula.

Lorena Melgarejo has worked as a community organizer for over 15 years, focusing her work in the immigrant community, developing their leadership to challenge and transform the shadow economy in which they live and work. Lorena currently holds a joint position with the Office of Public Policy and Social Concerns, Archdiocese of San Francisco, and SFOP/PIA. Throughout her career, she has worked with national, state, and local organizations for immigrant rights.

This essay is a reflection on our work in light of the vision of Pope Francis for a church of the poor and in response to Bishop McElroy's article, "A Church for the Poor."

Most of the people we accompany are immigrant workers who left Latin America to escape poverty, persecution, and violence. These workers are people of faith, hoping to find a place where they, along with their families and community, can be the participants of their own destiny. They see the United States of America as a country that could give them the means to satisfy their most basic human needs. However, their legal status, low levels of education, and poor English make them vulnerable to deportation, eviction, abuse, and exploitation. These injustices are the consequences of a system shaped by structural sin, as Bishop McElroy describes in his article.

Most of the excluded immigrants living in San Francisco escaped the physical experience of poverty, violence, and discrimination in their home countries, to then come to the United States and not be able to participate in the decisions that matter most to them. Specifically, as a result of international agreements, farm workers and other laborers make less money, lose their jobs, or agree to poor working contracts. Immigrants report that the influx of a deported gang culture into their countries has made the population more vulnerable to violence. Finally, the demand for drugs in the north led to drug cartels gaining control of cities and people to guarantee paths for the distribution of narcotics. Feeling hopeless in their own territory motivates immigrants to move north looking for a better life.

Many immigrants learned early in their lives that there are forces that determine a person's destiny and control all aspects of life. This way of reading the world makes people believe that they cannot participate in shaping society. In this sense, these immigrants operate within a state of mind that existed in Europe before the French Revolution. The European population believed that men and women did not create history; rather, the kings, as their representatives on earth, controlled their destinies. Experiences in Latin America have taught people that they do not exist without being controlled by the powerful systems and the people who control these systems. Coming from that reality makes it hard to accept the possibility of conceiving the world from a different perspective.

As organizers, we have learned that the system of exclusion does not readily tolerate pathways to inclusion; nevertheless, the immigrant population in the U.S. has hope that they can make a living. We have found that most of the excluded immigrants are not subversives. They do not want to change the system, but rather join the system. The problem with this approach is that marginalized immigrants exist in the United States outside the circle of human concern and protection. Consequently, they start believing that it is acceptable to lack access to certain benefits (healthcare, social security, affordable housing, a dignifying job, and so on). For those of us compelled by the Catholic social tradition, we cannot participate in such structures because in doing so, we permit and replicate injustices.

As organizers, we work with people who initially blame themselves for their own discomfort, rather than attributing it to unjust systems. This attitude is perpetuated by poverty, racism, and discrimination. Once the immigrant population realizes that they do not fit into the current model of progress, it becomes evident that the community needs to work for a different society. The challenge is to break away from the reality in which we are currently immersed by recognizing that history does not have a predetermined meaning and direction.

Our work has convinced us that we must be realistic and understand reality as both an articulation of what is given and an opportunity to participate in the creation of the world. Out of this conviction, we seek to go beyond an assimilation of reality, shaping it in areas where we see possible ways of acting. History has taught us that the world is captured in the act of participating as human beings, and a big challenge that we face in our community organizing efforts is convincing the Christian community to believe that immigrants can achieve their own autonomy.

Community organizing starts from the belief that there is an alternative to the great theory of the powerful; and it is rooted in the understanding that there is a force within our community that legitimizes us and motivates us to act differently. Once we re-interpret the immigrant experience and are able to criticize the unfair systems that keep people in the margins, we are able to question what it is obvious within the current system. This consciousness re-frames the socio-historical references from which immigrant families construct their knowledge, the way they see the world, and the way they want to actively participate in this world.

By raising consciousness, one recognizes injustices that support the marginalization of immigrants. In this system, discrimination is experienced as natural and presented as if the world should be that way. Capitalism thrives by exploiting vulnerable workers. It also perpetuates situations in which people cannot access their own rights. Specifically, many immigrants pay social security, but cannot access it; they work hard, but do not receive a fair wage; and when immigrants are deported, many employers do not send the salaries that they owe them. This system continues to subsidize the economic growth of the United States. The systemic tragedy is that this situation is still better than what people have experienced in their countries of origin. However, this reality does not justify a public policy that disregards the inalienable rights of the human person. The Catholic social tradition has explicitly denounced the systemic exploitation of immigrants:

> ...foreign [immigrant] workers, despite any difficulties concerning integration, make a significant contribution to the economic development of the host country through their labor, besides that which they make to their country of origin through the money they send home. Obviously, these laborers cannot be considered as a commodity or a mere workforce. They must not, therefore, be treated like any other factor of production. Every migrant is a human person who, as such, possesses fundamental, inalienable rights that must be respected by everyone and in every circumstance.[1]

Informed by our work and Catholic social thought, we believe that the current system of a globalized economy has to change. The economic system has facilitated progress for many people, but it cannot be sustained through history. Because we oppose inequality, we seek a progressive path that moves beyond the status quo into a different future. Social class, race, and gender are the main sources of inequality that the immigrant population experience. A tiered system that permits naming people as illegal or criminal for their immigration status creates a culture of indifference. There are people of good will all over the United States, but the trivialization of injustices makes people care about the problems immigrants face only for short periods of time. In other words, a culture of indifference makes people's sensitivity toward injustice short-lived. For this reason, it is so important to have the leadership of the Catholic Church speaking directly and frequently about the situation of the immigrant community in the United States. Their word is not only a word of authority that keeps the discussion going, but it also enables the immigrant community to participate in the transformation of the world in which we live. Latino immigrants tend to respond to the leadership of the Catholic Church. That is why we need priests to lead in education and promote the work for justice.

The Catholic faith becomes relevant particularly when the pope, and then the bishops, stand with the Latino community and connect the word of God with the experiences of immigration. It is an opportunity for people to unveil their own dignity that we are so eager to see. We need to see Catholic leadership in solidarity with the crucified people. Pope Francis expressed such solidarity when he visited a community of migrants on island of Lampedusa in 2013 and criticized the world for their indifference toward the migrants' suffering.

Charity is the usual language that we hear from the church, but the language of liberation to change structures of oppression does not have a prominent place in public discussions. Bringing this discussion forward is essential because Hispanic groups are usually conditioned to seek the authorization of our pope, the bishops, and priests. Within the current narrative of the church, we do not have permission to cry and complain about our own suffering. We are taught that we can complain about being sinners, but not about the realities of structural sin. The structure that makes us sin, like poverty, is not adequately addressed. Too often, the public discussion of the church makes us retreat into our own depression rather than participate in hope.

In current public Catholic discussions in the United States, it seems as though we received dignity from God at the moment of conception, but we lost it as soon as we were born in a poor foreign society. This needs to change, and it can only change if we know that our religious leaders are empowering us to change sinful structures. We need to know that we are allowed to respond to the suffering our community is enduring, and we need to be allowed to grieve and cry so the transformation of the system becomes part of the healing of the world. We need the church to be a place that reminds us of our dignity, so one can come out of church and transform the world.

When one embraces the belief that it is possible to change reality with a social movement, rather than accepting reality as naturally established, the discrimination of immigrants is historically possible to overcome. We doubt the status quo is static, and propose a praxis of transformation that is born from the experience of an immigrant Christian-based community. The pope's vision of a church of the poor and for the poor—and his powerful support of migrants around the world—is allowing our people to begin this transformation. We need the rest of the church to hear this narrative of hope and join us on the road of change.

That is the narrative that guides our work. The horizon that we have is inclusion because there is no growth without inclusion. The hope is to allow immigrant families to keep their families together, their homes, and their jobs. Honesty and hard work is what makes our community proud. We cannot allow the current Catholic conversation to tell us that our faith should focus on our guilt because, in our experience, that is what has made our community members become slaves to the system.

We are reclaiming people's dignity through faith-based organizing. Our experiences in Latin America have taught us already about human tragedy. Our people share stories of massacres, international delinquency, and persecution. We are a community of immigrants accompanying immigrants; undocumented people accompanying undocumented people. We feel angry about inequality, so we are committed to its elimination. God gave us permission to pray and act so the poor and undocumented can live a dignified life in the United States. Pope Francis is calling the whole church to remember this.

1   Pope Benedict XVI, Encyclical on Charity in Truth, *Caritas in Veritate* (2009), 62.

POPE FRANCIS, WOMEN, AND THE CHURCH FOR THE POOR

LISA FULLAM

Pope Francis has called for a fundamental shift in the pastoral emphasis of the church, calling leaders and laity alike to embrace Jesus's priority of welcoming the poor and the outcast. At the same time, Francis has spoken about women and women's roles in church and society in a way that is, at best, confusing. He calls for an increase of women's voice and authority, yet he undercuts that message when he addresses how that might work.

Here is the problem: the poor are disproportionately women and their dependent children. The Church of the Poor is a church in which women's voices must be heard and women's issues addressed—and the status quo is not working.

A POOR CHURCH ON THE SIDE OF THE POOR

The urgency with which Francis seeks to realign the church's mission on behalf of the poor has been clear from the start of his papacy.

Lisa Fullam teaches moral theology at the Jesuit School of Theology at Santa Clara University. Research interests include virtue ethics, medical and sexual ethics, the intersection of ethics and spirituality, and Ignatian spirituality. Published essays include: "Toward a Virtue Ethics of Marriage: Augustine and Aquinas on Friendship in Marriage," and "Why Ordination Matters: A Reflection from Jamaica." *Readings in Moral Theology #17, Ethics and Spirituality,* co-edited with Charles E. Curran, was published by Paulist Press in 2014 and her previous book, *The Virtue of Humility: A Thomistic Apologetic* was published by the Edwin Mellen Press in 2009.

He described his choice of papal moniker this way: "That is how the name came into my heart: Francis of Assisi. For me, he is the man of poverty, the man of peace . . . How I would like a Church which is poor and for the poor!"[1]

In his first major document, *Evangelii Gaudium* (EG),[2] Francis proposed "new paths for the Church's journey in years to come."[3] Selfish consumerism, he wrote, cuts those affected off from the poor: "Whenever our interior life becomes caught up in its own interests and concerns, there is . . . no place for the poor."[4] He attacked the "economy of exclusion" in stark terms:

> Such an economy kills . . . . Today everything comes under the laws of competition and the survival of the fittest, where the powerful feed upon the powerless. As a consequence, masses of people find themselves excluded and marginalized: without work, without possibilities, without any means of escape.[5]

An adequate response cannot be limited to personal acts of asceticism and charity.[6] Ultimately, Francis wrote, social policies that uphold inequality must be changed:

> We can no longer trust in the unseen forces and the invisible hand of the market. Growth in justice…requires decisions, programs, mechanisms and processes specifically geared to a better distribution of income, the creation of sources of employment and an integral promotion of the poor which goes beyond a simple welfare mentality.[7]

This emphasis on economic structural change to address poverty has alarmed many of the pope's conservative critics,[8] and at the same time, this focus on the poor has contributed considerably to Francis' popularity within and beyond the church.

POPE FRANCIS ON WOMEN

If Pope Francis' commitment to the poor has been clear and unwavering, his statements about women present a mixed message. At the level of generalities, he advocates powerfully for women; as to specifics, he argues mostly for the status quo, shored up by gender stereotypes.

Francis strongly affirms the equal dignity of women and men. In EG, he writes:

> Demands that the legitimate rights of women be respected, based on the firm conviction that men and women are equal in dignity, present the Church with profound and challenging questions which cannot be lightly evaded....[9]

He makes clear that this *does not* mean a change in women's official roles in the church: the bulk of this paragraph reiterates the church's exclusion of women from ordination. And while women are needed "where important decisions are made, both in the Church and in social structures,"[10] when he set up an unprecedented advisory board tasked with church reform, no women were deemed necessary.

This giving with one hand and taking away with the other is found throughout his papacy.[11] In an impromptu airplane interview, Francis called for a deeper theology of women, a theme he reiterated to several Jesuit-run publications later the same year.[12] In an address to participants in a conference on complementarity, he seemed to want to nuance the notion: "When we speak of complementarity between man and woman...we must not confuse the term with the simplistic idea that all the roles and relationships of both sexes are confined to a single and static model."[13] He called for equal pay for women and men (on grounds of complementarity), calling the wage gap "an absolute disgrace!"[14]

But when Francis writes about women, he employs the clichés of the Theology of the Body. In EG, he praises women for their "indispensable contribution" to society, but asserts that this is from a special "sensitivity" and "intuition" that women possess, not, e.g., for their intelligence, dedication, or skill.[15] Commenting on John Paul II's *Mulieris Dignitatem*, he lauds that document's "solid" anthropology, warning against "promoting a kind of emancipation that, in order to fill areas that have been taken away from the male, deserts the feminine attributes with all its precious characteristics."[16]

Those characteristics center on motherhood, which is far more than biological in scope: women who are not mothers are unfulfilled.

Using women as a metaphor for the church, he said that when the church does not evangelize, "she lacks joy, she lacks peace, and so she becomes a disheartened church, anxious, sad, a church that seems more like a spinster than a mother, and this church doesn't work.... The joy of the Church is to give birth.... "[17] Even celibate women are defined in maternal terms: "The consecrated woman is a mother, she must be a mother, not a 'spinster'!"[18]

Francis frequently uses language of sensitivity, intuition, and a related "feminine genius" in referring to women: "woman has a particular sensitivity to the 'things of God,' above all in helping us understand the mercy, tenderness and love that God has for us."[19] Even when he named an unprecedented five women to the International Theological Commission (calling them "the icing on the cake"[20]) he reiterated that the core of their "feminine genius" was their sensitivity and intuition—odd praise for academic theologians.

What about those expanded roles in the church? In May 2015, Pope Francis raised the tantalizing possibility of women leading curial dicasteries, saying "Yes, they can, in certain dicasteries they can; but what you are asking is simple functionalism."[21] He went on to describe women's true role is to act in accord with the "feminine genius." Intuition is key:

> When we face a problem among men we come to a conclusion, but when we face that same problem with women the outcome will be different. It will follow the same path, but it will be richer, stronger, more intuitive. For this reason women in the Church should have this role, they must clarify, help to clarify the feminine genius in so many ways.[22]

That sounds like an argument for women in high church positions, but a month later, Pope Francis slammed that door shut, saying that appointing women to dicastery leadership would be mere "functionalism,"[23] not a real advance for women.

In an interview with Jesuit publications, he warned against "'female *machismo*,' because a woman has a different make-up than a man."[24] And while it is important that women have greater opportunities in society, their real importance is in the home (a statement never made about men) because of their distinctively feminine traits: "[t]he gifts of refinement, particular sensitivity and tenderness, with which the woman's spirit is richly endowed..."[25] How to do both? He is not sure:

[H]ow can one increase an effective presence in so many areas of the public sphere...and at the same time maintain a presence and preferential and wholly special attention to the family? And this is the field for discernment which, in addition to the reflection on the reality of women in society, requires assiduous and persevering prayer.[26]

For Pope Francis, while things must change for women in the church and society, when it comes down to specifics he has little to suggest beyond equal pay. Women are defined by motherhood, literal and symbolic, and what is distinctive and necessary about women's participation in church and society is connected to a "feminine genius" that echoes John Paul II's sentimental and stereotypical vision of women. Women's first place is in the home. Reinscribing an unrevised complementarity as the norm for understanding women's roles and character, Francis has made clear that women's "equality" is theoretical, and their station is clearly secondary, defined in biological and emotional terms, and circumscribed by roles determined by men.

THE PROBLEM: THE POOR ARE WOMEN

Women are overrepresented among the poor. In the United States, 3.5 percent more women than men live in poverty, more than 1 in 7 women overall. At age 65 and over, the gap widens: 11.6 percent of women live in poverty, vs. 6.8 percent of men.[27] The poverty rate for female-headed (no adult male present) households with children is a stunning 30.6 percent.[28] The more than fourfold higher number of female-headed households over male-headed households means that the poverty gap is especially devastating for children: 19.9 percent of children in the United States—1 in 5—live in poverty.[29] More than half of all related children living in a female-headed household live in poverty.[30]

A number of factors conspire to trap women in poverty. Women earn less than men for their work.[31] Perhaps even more significantly, women tend to be shunted into lower-wage "pink collar" jobs;[32] 80 percent of workers in low-wage jobs are women.[33] Discriminatory or otherwise inadequate policies relating to family and child-care, along with the so-called "mommy tax"[34] further burden working women. Moreover, women are disproportionately counted on for low or unpaid care of children, people with disabilities, and dependent elders.[35]

The factors that drive women's greater poverty in the United States are present in the developing world, often to a greater degree.[36] The employment gap between men and women—13 percent in the developed world—reaches 28.1 percent in developing regions.[37] An education gap affects women: while parity between boys and girls has been achieved in primary education, and overall girls are not far behind boys in secondary education, substantial regional gaps persist.[38] The UN Women's Millennium Development Goals list a number of other factors that need attention internationally, including:

> …women's disproportionate share of unpaid care work, women's unequal access to assets, violations of women's and girls' sexual and reproductive health and rights, their unequal participation in private and public decision-making beyond national parliaments and violence against women and girls.[39]

UN Women marked the 20th anniversary of the Beijing Platform for action with these words:

> While both men and women suffer in poverty, gender discrimination means that women have far fewer resources to cope. They are likely to be the last to eat, the ones least likely to access healthcare, and routinely trapped in time-consuming, unpaid domestic tasks. They have more limited options to work or build businesses. Adequate education may lie out of reach. Some end up forced into sexual exploitation as part of a basic struggle to survive.[40]

While poverty assaults the human dignity of men and women, it is women who bear the brunt, both in numbers and in the social and public policy obstacles that differentially afflict women. To ignore the ways poverty specially targets women is to ignore the pervasive influence of the structural sin of sexism.

WHAT'S A POPE TO DO?

"Among our tasks as witnesses to the love of Christ is that of giving a voice to the cry of the poor."[41] Pope Francis has been eloquent and forceful in emphasizing the need for the ministry of the church to focus on the poor. Francis is not calling only for renewed acts of charity, but for a transformation of the structures that entrap the poor. However, when those structures are exposed, we see that women have been unequally victimized—the voice of the poor tends toward the treble end of the scale. As the Pope knows, confronting unjust social structures is a matter of deliberate empowerment of the marginalized. It is a matter, as he said, of "decisions, programs, mechanisms and processes" that address the structural roots of the evil.

Francis affirms the need for women's greater participation in decision-making in church and society. However, he undercuts that message by delimiting women's contributions, both in specific ways—e.g., they cannot be ordained, so are ineligible for the most ordinary form of servant leadership in the church[42]—and also by repeating unchanged the formulations about women that justify their marginalization. Women are lauded for maternity, not political savvy, for intuition, not intellectual acuity. Their most important role is at home, not in Congress, parliament, or on the papal advisory committee.

He cannot have it both ways. Either he must abandon his hope for a true church for the poor, or he must address with clarity and specificity ways in which women may be empowered in church and society. To continue the status quo will render his dream for the church a mirage, or, worse, a cynical stance that affirms women with one hand while holding them back with the other. To confront the structures of sexism that afflict men and women requires courage: It is the courage to listen with an open heart to the experience of women. It is the courage to name and redress historical and contemporary acts of violence against women, and to name and eliminate the structures that justify that violence. It is to invite women to take their rightful place alongside their brothers in the church and in society, not as "icing on the cake," but as collaborators in the work of the kingdom of God. It is to trust in the spirit of God that She will be with us always, leading us, consoling us, and encouraging us as we work for the justice in the world for which Jesus lived and died and lives anew.

1   Pope Francis, Address of the Holy Father (March 16, 2013), accessed May 26, 2015, https://w2.vatican.va/content/francesco/en/speeches/2013/march/documents/papa-francesco_20130316_rappresentanti-media.html, Francis also noted his namesake's care for creation, an emphasis he explored in his encyclical *Laudato Si'*.

2   The first encyclical issued under his signature, *Lumen Fidei*, was drafted in Pope Benedict XVI's pontificate; that encyclical's reflection on faith completed Benedict's writing on the theological virtues started with *Spes Salvi* (2007) and *Caritas in Veritate* (2009). *Evangelii Gaudium* is Pope Francis' first major document.

3   Pope Francis, Apostolic Exhortation on the Proclamation of the Gospel in Today's World, *Evangelii Gaudium* (2013), 1. Cited hereafter as EG.

4   Ibid., 2.

5   Ibid., 53.

6   While personal steps *alone* are inadequate, Pope Francis does call for personal as well as political action: "Poverty today is a cry. We must all think about whether we can become a little poorer." His own example underscores that message: this is the pope who travels in a Ford Focus and lives in a Vatican guesthouse. Pope Francis, "Address of Pope Francis to the Students of the Jesuit Schools of Italy and Albania," Q&A (June 7, 2013), accessed May 27, 2015, https://w2.vatican.va/content/francesco/en/speeches/2013/june/documents/papa-francesco_20130607_scuole-gesuiti.html.

7   EG, 204.

8   Two quick examples: rightwing provocateur Rush Limbaugh called him a Marxist, (http://www.rushlimbaugh.com/daily/2013/11/27/it_s_sad_how_wrong_pope_francis_is_unless_it_s_a_deliberate_mistranslation_by_leftists, accessed 5/27/15,) while blogger and former White House speechwriter Mark W. Davis at US News and World Report labeled him dangerously naïve, (http://www.usnews.com/opinion/blogs/mark-davis/2015/05/27/pope-francis-naive-views-on-poverty-and-capitalism-are-dangerous.)

9   EG, 104.

10 Ibid., 103.

11 For a useful and pointed summary, see Miriam Duignan, "In His Thoughts and in His Words. Francis on Women," in *Conscience* XXXV, no 4 (2014): 19-23.

12 Antonio Spadaro, S.J., "A Big Heart Open to God," *America* magazine (September 30, 2013), accessed June 3, 2015, http://americamagazine.org/pope-interview. Jesuit Tom Reese said this meant that: "Pope Francis threw John Paul's theology of women under the bus." Thomas Reese, "Where Pope Francis Stands When it Comes to Women," in *National Catholic Reporter* (March 20, 2015), accessed June 1, 2015, http://ncronline.org/blogs/faith-and-justice/where-pope-francis-stands-when-it-comes-women.

13 Pope Francis, "Address of His Holiness Pope Francis to Participants in the International Colloquium on the Complementarity Between Man and Woman Sponsored by the Congregation for the Doctrine of the Faith," (November 17, 2014), accessed June 26, 2015, https://w2.vatican.va/content/francesco/en/speeches/2014/november/documents/papa-francesco_20141117_congregazione-dottrina-fede.html.

14 Pope Francis, General Audience (April 29, 2015), accessed June 26, 2015 https://w2.vatican.va/content/francesco/en/audiences/2015/documents/papa-francesco_20150429_udienza-generale.html.

15 EG, 103.

16 Pope Francis, Address to Participants in a Seminar Organized by the Pontifical Council for the Laity on the Occasion of the 25th Anniversary of *Mulieris Dignitatem* (October 12, 2013), accessed July 28, 2015, http://m.vatican.va/content/francesco/en/speeches/2013/october/documents/papa-francesco_20131012_seminario-xxv-mulieris-dignitatem.pdf.

17 Pope Francis, Homily at Morning Mass (Dec 9, 2014), quoted by David Gibson, "Seven Pope Francis Quotes That Make Women Wince," in *Huffington Post Religion*, (June 1, 2015), accessed June 3, 2015, http://www.huffingtonpost.com/2014/12/11/pope-francis-women_n_6307822.html.

18 Pope Francis, "Address of Pope Francis to the Participants in the Plenary Assembly of the International Union of Superiors General, (I.U.S.G.)" (May 8, 2013), accessed June 3, 2015, https://w2.vatican.va/content/francesco/en/speeches/2013/may/documents/papa-francesco_20130508_uisg.html. He does not use language of lack of human fulfillment of men who, like himself, forego fatherhood, nor does he warn celibate men to avoid the masculine equivalent of spinsterhood.

19 Pope Francis, "Address to Participants in a Seminar Organized by the Pontifical Council for the Laity on the Occasion of the 25th Anniversary of *Mulieris Dignitatem*." That special sensitivity for the things of God, helping people understand God's mercy and care, is a curious quality to laud in people barred from priesthood.

20 Pope Francis, "Address of His Holiness Pope Francis to members of the

International Theological Commission," (December 5, 2014), accessed June 3, 2015, https://w2.vatican.va/content/francesco/en/speeches/2014/december/documents/papa-francesco_20141205_commissione-teologica-internazionale.html. Women now make up 16% of the members of the ITC.

21 Pope Francis, "Address of His Holiness Pope Francis to Consecrated Men and Women of the Diocese of Rome," (May 16, 2015), accessed June 26, 2015, http://www.news.va/en/news/to-religious-people-of-the-diocese-of-rome-16-may.

22 Ibid. In regard to the nature of the feminine genius, he spoke of a nun's smile, and of patience in community life.

23 Joshua J. McElwee, "Francis Again Rejects Women as Heads of Vatican Offices," in *National Catholic Reporter* (June 21, 2015), accessed June 26, 2015, http://ncronline.org/news/vatican/francis-again-rejects-women-heads-vatican-offices. So what, exactly is "functionalism" for Francis? In an address to the participants in the general assembly of the Pontifical Missionary Societies, he warned participants not to become like NGO's, not to put functionalism at the center of their work, but instead the spirit of Christ. (News.va, June 5, 2015 http://www.news.va/en/news/pontifical-missionary-societies-opening-up-to-geog, accessed June 26, 2015). In other words, if they do their work absent a vibrant connection to Jesus, they are merely acting out their role, not fully living it. It is not clear how this use applies to women in Vatican leadership, unless exercising ecclesial leadership—something Francis has called for—inherently contradicts the "feminine genius."

24 Spadaro, "A Big Heart Open to God." Francis seems to engage in a kind of thinking critiqued by early feminists, who noted that whenever women wanted to expand their range into areas traditionally restricted to men, (by men,) they were accused of wanting to be men.

25 Pope Francis, "Address of Pope Francis to the Participants in the National Congress Sponsored by the Italian Women's Center," (January 25, 2014), accessed June 3, 2015, http://w2.vatican.va/content/francesco/en/speeches/2014/january/documents/papa-francesco_20140125_centro-italiano-femminile.html..

26 Ibid.

27 Joan Entmacher, Katherine Gallagher Robbins, Julie Vogtman, and Anne Morrison, National Women's Law Center, Insecure and Unequal. Poverty and Income among Women and Families, 2000-2013 (Washington D.C.: NWLC, 2014), 1, accessed June 5, 2015, http://www.nwlc.org/sites/default/files/pdfs/final_2014_nwlc_poverty_report.pdf. While not my topic here, it must not be forgotten that race matters, too: black, Hispanic and Native American women have poverty rates about three times higher than that of white non-Hispanic men.

28 DeNavas-Walt, Carmen and Bernadette D. Proctor, U.S. Census Bureau, Current Population Reports, P60-249, *Income and Poverty in the United States:*

2013, U.S. Government Printing Office, Washington, DC, 2014, pg. 15-16.

29 Ibid., 14.

30 Ibid.

31 AAUW, *The Simple Truth about the Gender Pay Gap*, (Washington, D.C.: AAUW, 2015), 3. The statistical benchmark here is women's vs. men's median earnings for full-time work, overall. The wage gap also exacerbated by race for most groups.

32 Trond Petersen and Laurie A. Morgan, "Separate and Unequal: Occupation-Establishment Sex Segregation and the Gender Wage Gap," *The American Journal of Sociology*, Vol. 101, No. 2 (Sep., 1995): 329-365. This paper compares people in similar jobs, and corrects for a number of variables not accounted for in the blunter comparison of women's vs. men's median earnings.

33 Bread for the World, "Hunger and Poverty among Women and Children," (Washington, D.C.: 2014), accessed June 5, 2015, http://www.bread.org/media/pdf/women-children-us-2014.pdf.

34 Justine Calcagno, "The 'Mommy Tax' and 'Daddy Bonus.' Parenthood and Income in New York City 1990-2010" Center for Latin American, Caribbean & Latino Studies Graduate Center, CUNY (May, 2014), accessed June 5, 2014, http://www.gc.cuny.edu/CUNY_GC/media/CUNY-Graduate-Center/PDF/Centers/CLACLS/Parenthood-and-Income-in-New-York-City-1990-2010.pdf.

35 Nancy Folbre, ed., *For Love and Money: Care Provision in the United States*, (New York: Russell Sage Foundation, 2012), xi.

36 The oft-cited "70% of the world's poor are women" lacks substantiation. In part, little data exists to address the question directly. For example, when studies focus on numbers of poor families, it is hard to distinguish upon the distribution of goods within families. Even studies that assert (apparently also without data,) that men and women are equally represented among the poor point to differential structural disadvantages facing women. See Pedro Olinto, Kathleen Beegle, Carlos Sobrado, and Hiroki Uematsu, "The State of the Poor: Where Are The Poor, Where Is Extreme Poverty Harder to End, and What Is the Current Profile of the World's Poor?," Poverty Reduction and Economic Management Network, The World Bank (October, 2013), accessed June 6, 2015, http://siteresources.worldbank.org/EXTPREMNET/Resources/EP125.pdf.

37 United Nations Statistics Division, UN Women, "Millennium Development Goals. Gender Chart. Special edition for the 58th session of the Commission on the Status of Women, New York, Goal 1," (10-21 March 2014), accessed June 5, 2015, http://www.unwomen.org/~/media/headquarters/attachments/sections/library/publications/2014/gender%20gap%202014%20for%20web%20pdf.ashx.

38 Sub-Saharan Africa is the worst region for girls' secondary education, with a gender parity index of 0.83. United Nations Statistics Division, UN Women, "Millennium Development Goals. Gender Chart. Special edition for the 58th session of the Commission on the Status of Women, New York, Goal 2," (10-

21 March 2014), accessed June 6, 2015, http://www.unwomen.org/~/media/
headquarters/attachments/sections/library/publications/2014/gender%20
gap%202014%20for%20web%20pdf.ashx.

39 United Nations Statistics Division, UN Women, "Millennium Development
    Goals. Gender Chart. Special edition for the 58th session of the Commission
    on the Status of Women, New York, Goal 3," (10-21 March 2014), accessed
    June 6, 2015, http://www.unwomen.org/~/media/headquarters/attachments/
    sections/library/publications/2014/gender%20gap%202014%20for%20
    web%20pdf.ashx.

40 UN Women, "Women and Poverty," *Beijing 20*, accessed June 6, 2015, http://
    beijing20.unwomen.org/en/for-later/poverty.

41 Pope Francis, "Address of Holy Father Francis to His Grace Justin Welby,
    Archbishop of Canterbury and Primate of the Anglican Communion," (June
    14, 2013), accessed June 6, 2015, https://w2.vatican.va/content/francesco/en/
    speeches/2013/june/documents/papa-francesco_20130614_welby-canterbury.
    html.

42 Interestingly, by ruling out women's ordination Francis leaves himself with a
    far more difficult problem. For women to have real voice in the church without
    admitting them into the structures of leadership that exist now would require
    a near-total reordering of the hierarchical structure of church leadership. Lay
    people, for example, would need to be able to contribute with vote as well
    as voice in decisions on doctrinal matters, and perhaps on priest-personnel
    decisions as well. Ordaining women would seem to be the LESS radical change
    Francis could make to include women meaningfully in the leadership of the
    church.

POPE FRANCIS, INCLUSIVENESS, AND THE LGBT COMMUNITY

BRIAN CAHILL

Bishop Robert McElroy has advocated strongly and eloquently that his fellow bishops should give the same priority to poverty and inequality that they give to issues regarding sexuality. He is right, but the issue is not just the obsession of some bishops in the area of sexuality, but also how disrespectful and insensitive some bishops have been in their treatment of gays and lesbians and transgender people.

I am the father of a gay son and I was slow to learn how painful, denigrating, and debilitating were the constant legal, social, and religious reminders that he and those like him were not fully accepted members of the human community. In *Hidden*, Richard Giannone writes about his experience as a young gay Catholic: "The lesson of alienation comes easily to a malleable young consciousness and stays. The cumulative effect is toxic. The pain is insupportable."[1]

The cumulative effect for my son was toxic and the pain was insupportable. Years later my son would tell me about being a terrified

Brian Cahill retired in 2009 as the Executive Director of San Francisco Catholic Charities after a 40-year career in social services. He is a husband, father, and grandfather. He is a volunteer suicide prevention trainer for the San Francisco Police Department and a volunteer in prison ministry at San Quentin Prison. His writing on public policy and religion has been published in the *San Francisco Chronicle* and *National Catholic Reporter*.

fourteen-year-old, realizing he was gay, not knowing what to do about it, completely frightened and feeling no security or support from his mother or from me. When I recall that time in the early eighties, I think I knew my son was gay before he did. But I did not have a clue how to talk about it with him or what to do about it. At the time, I figured if I loved him enough he would be okay. It never occurred to me then that he would not feel safe and protected by that love. I was also abysmally ignorant of how much he would be on the receiving end of hate and ignorance in the world—hate and ignorance for the most part that derives from organized religion.

Many bishops appear to ignore recent scholarship regarding same-sex relations. In *Confronting Power and Sex in the Catholic Church*, Australian Bishop Geoffrey Robinson argues that there is no possibility of a change in church teaching on homosexual acts unless the church changes its teaching on heterosexual acts. Citing the church's claim that God inserted into nature the demand that every human sexual act be both unitive and procreative, he contends that this teaching creates the false image of an angry, sex-obsessed God, and he reminds us that the teaching is simply an assertion with no compelling arguments or proof that it reflects God's will. Robinson proposes that the church consider sexual acts in relation to the good or harm done to individuals and their relationships rather than in terms of offending God. He believes the sexual act should be motivated by a desire for what is good in the other person, should involve no coercion or deceit, and should not harm a third party. He believes these requirements can be better met in marriage, but he does not believe that is the only way they can be met. Robinson suggests that either heterosexual or homosexual acts, if they meet these requirements, are not offensive to God, but are rather pleasing because they enhance individuals and relationships.[2]

In a recent book, *God and the Gay Christian*, Matthew Vines, a young gay evangelical, makes a compelling case for affirming orthodox, scripture-based faith and at the same time affirming committed same-sex relationships. With scholarship and clarity he refutes and discredits the well-known passages in Genesis, Leviticus,

Romans, 1 Corinthians, and 1 Timothy that have been the basis of church teaching on homosexuality.[3] Vines goes on to say,

> When we tell people that their every desire for intimate, sexual bonding is shameful and disordered, we encourage them to hate a core part of who they are. And when we reject the desire of gay Christians to express their sexuality within a lifelong covenant, we separate them from our covenantal God, and we tarnish their ability to bear his image.[4]

I wish these authors had been around years ago. I might have done a better job in supporting my son. But I have always known that my son is made in the image and likeness of God. He is certainly not objectively disordered and he should not be anything less than a fully accepted member of our human community.

Today I am no longer groveling in guilt. I love my son and he knows it. I am proud of him and he knows that. I respect his intellect, his integrity, his endurance, his professional accomplishments, and his 10-year committed relationship with his partner. But I cannot rewrite history. I know the implications, the outcomes of my failure—the reality that while we love each other, there is tension in the relationship. There is complexity in the relationship. There are scars in the relationship—scars not easily removed.

Just as I traveled a long road in learning what it meant to love my gay son, so, it seems to me, do some bishops need to travel this road in learning to love all of our gay and lesbian brothers and sisters. They need to internalize the spirit of Pope Francis' now famous statement, "Who am I to judge?" San Francisco Archbishop Salvatore Cordileone continues to lead the church's failed effort against civil same-sex marriage and against workplace protection for gays and lesbians. Cordileone repeatedly proclaims that children need a mother and a father, ignoring both the heterosexual divorce rate and the thousands of children in the foster care system, placed there because of the neglect or abuse of their heterosexual parents—parents who are living proof that sexual orientation is not a reliable indicator of good parenting. He also ignores that the only significant cohort of adoptive parents for the most vulnerable of these children are qualified gay and lesbian couples who want to form family. Finally he ignores that many children, when they leave the foster care system, struggle with poverty and homelessness as young adults.

For almost ten years as the Executive Director of San Francisco Catholic Charities, I was directly involved in efforts to manage the tension between what our church taught in the area of sexuality, and how we carried out our mission to serve the poor, the vulnerable, and the marginalized. We dealt with many challenges, but the most complex, significant, and painful issue was adoption by same-sex parents. The focus of the Catholic Charities adoption program was finding suitable placements for foster care children. In recent years, we averaged 25 adoptions per year. Few same-sex couples applied, but when they did, we were pleased to work with them if they met the criteria.

In June 2003, the Congregation for the Doctrine of the Faith issued an updated teaching on gay marriage. For the first time, same-sex adoption was prohibited and same-sex adoptive parents were characterized as "doing violence" to children by adopting them. My boss, Archbishop William Levada, was a member of the Congregation at that time, but he never directed me to stop working with same-sex adoptive couples. In late 2005, *The Boston Globe* reported that Boston Catholic Charities had been placing children with same-sex couples. In light of the Vatican directive, Boston decided to end their adoption program in early March 2006. *The Boston Globe* began to look at San Francisco, and as a result, Archbishop Levada, now in Rome, issued a statement acknowledging that I told him about a few cases of hard-to-place children with same-sex couples. He stated "these placements involved prudential judgments about the needs of the children, the teachings of the Catholic church, and the overall policies of Catholic Charities." He went on to state that since the 2003 Vatican statement, "it has been and remains my position that Catholic agencies should not place children in homosexual households."

When George Niederauer replaced Levada as archbishop, he took a pastoral approach in addressing this issue and allowed us to develop a strategy that would not conflict with church teaching and at the same time allow us to continue to serve these vulnerable children. We created a work group of program staff, board members, health care ethicists, and two highly qualified priest theologians. We began to work with Family Builders, a local adoption agency with rich experience recruiting same-sex couples as adoptive parents. Family Builders also had developed a statewide adoption match website called California Kids' Connection. There was limited funding for the website, and as a result, county adoption agencies were not using it. Our employees would transition over to Family Builders and staff the website. They would answer questions from prospective adoptive parents about specific children, and would help families find an adoption agency in their area so they could begin the adoption process.

Because our staff would not do specific matching or placing, our consulting theologians determined there would be no formal cooperation with evil. While I did not consider anything we were doing to be *evil*, I understood the need to be clear that we were not in conflict with church teaching. The archbishop approved the program and our board approved $250,000 annually for the staff allocation and related costs. Our workers on the website responded to more than 400 inquiries per month, resulting in 40 adoptions a year.

When the collaboration was announced, we had a positive response from our local government partners and from the secular press, but the reaction of the conservative Catholic press was scathing. In spite of the archbishop's support of the program, there was strong conservative pressure to end the program, which happened when I retired at the end of 2008. Based on a poorly conceived, disrespectful, and harshly written Roman policy, San Francisco Catholic Charities joined Boston, New York, Chicago, Washington, and other dioceses abandoning a 100-year tradition and thousands of poor and needy children.

Today, it is impossible to ignore the impact of Pope Francis who tells his bishops to stop being obsessed with the sexuality issues and who sees his role as pastor, compassionate friend, and fellow sinner on the Christian journey. The Vatican Synod on the Family convened by Pope Francis, opened with refreshing sense of inclusiveness, sensitivity, and respect for homosexuals. Halfway through the session, conservatives were fighting back hard, resisting any change in church teaching. Between the start and close of the Synod, language changes give a hint of what is to come. The phrase "welcoming homosexual persons" was dialed back to the more antiseptic "giving pastoral attention to persons with homosexual tendencies." In late May of this year, the pope's hand-picked Secretary of State, Cardinal Pietro Parolin, characterized the Irish vote approving same-sex marriage as "a defeat for humanity." And in June, Francis felt compelled to stress the importance of children having heterosexual parents.

So how are we to see this pope? Clearly he is a breath of fresh air, committed to transparency and a reform of the Roman institutional structure. He may not initiate any change in doctrine, but hopefully he is laying the groundwork for changes in the future. It is certainly possible that the hardliners in the Vatican—especially the young ones—are simply waiting him out with the hope of replacing him with one of their own. But I think it is also possible that this pope, with his modeling a spirit of simplicity, compassion, and love at the highest levels of the church, is reminding all of us—lay people, clergy, religious, and especially bishops—that there must be a balance between law and love, that the law is to serve love and cannot be considered as an end itself. And the pope's actions and words from day one make his pastoral approach and his commitment to inclusiveness crystal clear.

But the hardliners—those who prioritize the law over love—are not slowing down. San Francisco Archbishop Cordileone is attempting to enforce Catholic identity, which he measures all but exclusively in terms of sexual ethics in Catholic high schools, and weaken teacher employment rights. Moreover, one can look around the country to see multiple cases of gay and lesbian teachers being fired—good and dedicated teachers, who kept their private life separate from their work life and who would never consider undermining their schools or in any way harming their students.

Pope Francis may not be changing church doctrine, but he has moved the entire world with his compassion and his inclusiveness. This is a man who knows how to teach. This is a man with moral authority. It is worth noting that some bishops reflect the spirit of

Francis. Archbishop Cupich preaches that respect for gay people must be real and not just rhetorical, and Bishop McElroy calls for banishing judgmentalism from our church. But others appear to have their own agenda of judgment, condemnation, and exclusiveness. It is not the agenda of the U.S. Supreme Court or the agenda of most Catholics. It is not the agenda of Pope Francis and it is not consistent with the message of Jesus.

1   Richard Giannone, *Hidden, Reflections on Gay Life, AIDS and Spiritual Desire* (New York: Fordham University Press, 2012), 9.

2   Geoffrey Robinson, *Confronting Power and Sex in the Catholic Church* (Mulgrave Australia: John Garratt Publishing, 2007), 201-213.

3   Matthew Vines, *God and the Gay Christian, the Biblical Case in Support of Same-Sex Relationships* (New York: Convergent Books, 2014), 59-116.

4   Ibid., 158.

SOCIAL SIN, ECONOMIC INEQUALITY, AND THE COMMON GOOD

KRISTIN E. HEYER

Whereas narratives blaming individual "thuggish looters" in Baltimore or "willful lawbreakers" in southern Arizona frequently prevail in the American media, the Catholic tradition underscores social dimensions of justice and sinful complicity alike. Pope Francis tweets it plainly: "inequality is the root of social evil." As he elaborates in *Evangelii Gaudium*, "As long as the problems of the poor are not radically resolved by rejecting the absolute autonomy of markets and financial speculation and by attacking the structural causes of inequality, no solution will be found for the world's problems…"[1] Echoing the core understanding of justice in the Catholic social tradition as meaningful participation, the pope repeatedly underscores the impact of economies of exclusion and myriad forms of marginalization. Yet as Bishop Robert McElroy has lamented, the pope's diagnosis has not been welcomed by many American Catholics who criticize it as radical, simplistic, or misplaced. The cultural assumptions fueling such resistance— whether the sacralization of free markets or a zero sum game

Kristin E. Heyer is professor of theology at Boston College. She recently taught at Santa Clara and Loyola Marymount universities in California. Her most recent book is *Kinship Across Borders: A Christian Ethic of Immigration* (Georgetown University Press, 2012).

between makers and takers[2]—bid us to join economic analyses with sustained attention to the dynamics of social sin.

Over 45 million Americans live in poverty, while the richest one percent own more wealth than the bottom 90 percent. With the world's largest economy, the United States has the second highest child poverty rate among 35 industrialized countries. Not only is the discrepancy between CEO and average worker pay in the United States considerable, the gap is 10 times larger than typical Americans' perceptions: a 2014 study found the median American respondent estimated the ratio of CEO to worker income at 30 to 1, whereas the ratio is more than 350 to 1.[3] Such misperceptions reduce residents' desire to take action to counteract the discrepancy. Whereas other developed countries have used government policy to counteract inequality, the United States has adopted tax, wage, and financial policies that further intensify inequality.[4] The Catholic social tradition cautions that polarizing wealth disparities violate not only basic principles of justice but also concentrate power in ways that threaten social cohesion and democratic integrity.[5]

Recent events across the U.S. make painfully clear the links between economic inequality and broader disenfranchisement and its consequences. At the same time, the globalization of neoliberal capitalism has contributed to transnational inequalities issuing desperate efforts for basic survival. During his first official trip outside Rome to Lampedusa, Pope Francis commemorated in ritual and word the then-estimated 20,000 African immigrants who had died over the past 25 years trying to reach a new life in Europe (two years later, the latest capsized boat carrying migrants across the Mediterranean has left hundreds more feared drowned). Pope Francis' 2013 homily there within sight of the "graveyard of wrecks" noted the pervasive idolatry that facilitates migrants' deaths and robs us of the ability to weep. Amid his admission that even he remains "disoriented," he did not merely condemn "the world" for this indifference and its consequences, but repented: "Forgive us Lord!" whether for being closed in on our own well-being in a way that leads to anesthesia of the heart, or making global decisions creating situations that lead to these tragedies. The pope's reflections remind us that naming the reality of sin helps shed light on the structures and attitudes that harm refugees—and so many other victims of "a throwaway culture." Yet many Christians resist a deeper ethic of solidarity, susceptible as we remain to various disvalues.

Again in his 2015 Lenten message—may we "become islands of mercy in a sea of indifference"—Pope Francis signals how challenging economic inequalities must extend beyond meeting needs and crafting policies to healing social sin. Identifying and countering structural injustices and the ideologies that legitimatize them constitute a key contribution to pursuing the global common good. Various levels of social sin intersect in complex manners: pervasive, internalized ideologies make us susceptible to myths; operative understandings influence our actions or inaction. When bias hides or skews values, it becomes more difficult to choose authentic values over those that prevail in society, a tendency already present because of original sin.

Such intersections with respect to the global economy have been of particular concern to Pope Francis. Warning that our "economy of exclusion and inequality kills," he rightly challenges not only the reductive market ethos dominating trade and migration policies but also their desensitizing effects: "The culture of prosperity deadens us; we are thrilled if the market offers us something new to purchase; and in the meantime, all those lives stunted for lack of opportunity seem a mere spectacle; they fail to move us."[6] The elevation of wealth and influence to absolute status can become an authentic bondage. Idolatries focused on having over being can impede pursuit of the common good as much as nationalistic ones: they shape loyalties, frame questions, inform votes and spending practices.

Hence distinct elements of social sin—dehumanizing trends, unjust structures, and harmful ideologies—shape complex dynamics at play in perpetuating inequalities. To take the immigration example prompted by Lampedusa, the primacy of deterrence has institutionalized security concerns rather than concerns for human rights or family unity in U.S. immigration laws; the nation's economic interests have been institutionalized in uneven free trade agreements. When concerns about our identity get distorted by xenophobia and fear, anti-immigrant sentiment and ethnic-based hate crimes surge. At a more subtle level, a consumerist ideology shapes citizens' willingness to underpay or mistreat migrant laborers either directly or through indirect demand for inexpensive goods and services. These interconnected attitudes and institutions then produce the blindness that lulls us into equating "law-abiding" with "just" or into apathetic acquiescence. Consider other examples: The siting of toxic waste dumps in politically and economically powerless communities ensues not only due to histories of redlining culpable real estate agents or city council members but also due to our (not always conscious) desire to live near people who look and think and spend like us. Proponents of "virtuous capitalism" who fail to interrogate more structural causes of poverty obscure these dynamics of sin as they obstruct social justice.

Neoliberal globalization's operative priorities are often internalized in ways that shape the perceptions and actions of the dominant culture. Whether in fatalistic understandings of the "price of progress" or the "neutrality" of the market system, these more ideological currents of globalization configure our coordinates for what becomes conceivable.[7] Bishop McElroy has noted how the tendency in U.S. culture to understand the freedom of the markets as a categorical imperative rather than instrumental good can blind us to the gospel's demands. George Soros terms U.S. society's dominant belief system "Market Fundamentalism;" others refer to a "gospel of consumption" driving certain modes of globalization. Various commitments to growth at all costs can become authentic bondage that contributes to scotosis. In Pope Francis' words, "An economic system centered on the god of money also needs to plunder nature in order to maintain the frenetic pace of consumption inherent in it."[8]

These entrenched, intertwined patterns of social sin require repentance from idolatries that marginalize and disempower those beyond our immediate spheres of concern and borders. From repentance and conscientization we are called to conversion toward interdependence in solidarity. In contrast to a narrative of the self-made person, a Christian understanding of ourselves as freely "gifted" can motivate actions that enact gratuity in response. Such metanoia can occur through personal encounters and relationships that provoke new perspectives and receptivity. At the broader systemic level, nations must understand themselves as collectively responsible for the shared challenges posed by environmental devastation, the arms market, and migrant deaths.

Pope John Paul II forwarded solidarity as the key virtue demanded in a globalized era of de facto interdependence: "the social face of Christian love."[9] David Hollenbach proposes institutional solidarity as a necessary means of moving patterns of global interdependence from ones marked by domination and oppression to ones marked by equality and reciprocity. Institutional solidarity demands the development of structures that offer marginalized persons a genuine voice in the decisions and policies that impact their lives.[10] Due to the fact that much of the planet experiences marginalization, or at least "economic development takes place over their heads,"[11] a meaningful recovery of the sense that persons who are poor or on the move are *agents* rather than beneficiaries of charitable assistance or paternalist reforms remains essential. Hence institutional solidarity demands the inclusion of comprehensive sets of stakes at the decision-making table, structures of institutional accountability and transparency, and empowered participation (subsidiarity).[12] Realizing a truly global common good must robustly engage women, given the feminization of poverty and of migration across the globe and our incomplete agency in the world church.

In light of the depth and lure of sinful resistance to the steep challenge global solidarity imparts, two additional dimensions of solidarity are required: incarnational and conflictual solidarities. Given the grip of egotism in our soap bubbles of indifference, some observers have described the reception of recent Catholic teaching on solidarity as superficial or non-existent. Incarnational solidarity departs from valuable intellectual and institutional dimensions of solidarity to immerse our bodies and expend precious energy in practices of concrete accompaniment in the real world. Christine Firer Hinze's evocative metaphors for the reach of consumerism reflect the dynamics of social sin: a culture whose "kudzu-like values and practices so crowd the landscape of daily lives that solidarity finds precious little ground in which to take root."[13] She highlights consumerist culture's use of seduction and misdirection to "lay a soothing, obfuscating mantle over systemic injustices that solidarity would expose, [as] its participants are fitted with Oz-like lenses, fed a stream of distractions and novelties, and situated in a 24/7 schedule of work-spend-consume that virtually ensures they will 'pay no attention' to the suffering multitudes behind the curtain."[14] Given the interconnection between unjust international structures in need of reform and these pervasive ideologies, an "incarnational" solidarity like Hinze has proposed complements the institutional solidarity advanced above.

In closing, promoting solidarity among institutions and persons cannot bypass conflict and loss. Liberation theologians and social ethicists have noted magisterial Catholicism's tendency to prioritize unity, harmony, and synthesis in ways that circumvent necessary conflict. Without confronting issues of economic and political power and engaging grassroots mobilization, work toward and implementation of changes to the status quo will remain stunted; contesting inequalities also requires a tolerance for disagreement and may entail lament or righteous anger—in short, the recalcitrance of the privileged may demand a more "conflictual solidarity" as well.

For even remaining adrift in a sea of indifference is a privilege. May the church cultivate solidarities that "heal the wounds" of social sin that threaten our common good.

1   Pope Francis, Apostolic Exhortation on the Proclamation of the Gospel in Today's World, *Evangelii Gaudium* (2013), 202. Cited hereafter as EG.

2   Most Rev. Robert W. McElroy, "Pope Francis' challenge to income inequality," *America* (November 3, 2014).

3   David Sirota, "Americans unaware of staggering gap between rich and poor," *San Francisco Chronicle* (October 2, 2014).

4 David Carroll Cochran, "Plutocracy or Democracy? How Bad Policies Brought Us a New Gilded Age," *Commonweal* (February 10, 2012): 7-9 at 9.

5 Cochran, 7.

6 EG, 54.

7 Timothy Jarvis Gorringe, "Invoking: Globalization and Power," in *The Blackwell Companion to Christian Ethics*, ed. Stanley Hauerwas and Samuel Wells (Malden, MA: Blackwell Publishing Ltd, 2004), 346-59 at 353.

8 Francis X. Rocca, "Pope urges activists to struggle against 'structural causes' of poverty," *Catholic News Service* available at http://www.catholicnews.com/data/stories/cns/1404449.htm.

9 John Paul II, Encyclical on the Social Concern of the Church, *Solicitudo rei socialis* (1987), 40.

10 David Hollenbach, S.J., "The Life of the Human Community," *America* (November 4, 2002): 6-9 at 7.

11 Pope John Paul II, Encyclical on the Hundredth Anniversary of Rerum Novarum, *Centesimus Annus* (1991) in *Catholic Social Thought: The Documentary Heritage*, ed. David J O'Brien and Thomas A. Shannon (Maryknoll, NY: Orbis, 1998) no. 33, 463.

12 Hollenbach, *Common Good & Christian Ethics* (Cambridge Mass.: Cambridge University Press, 2002), 225.

13 Christine Firer Hinze, "Straining Toward Solidarity in a Suffering World: Gaudium et spes 'After Forty Years,'" in *Vatican II: Forty Years Later, College Theology Society Annual Volume 51*, ed. William Madges (2005), 165-95 at 180.

14 Ibid., 181-82.

VOTER SUPPRESSION AS A PRIORITY: FIGHTING DISENFRANCHISEMENT (YET AGAIN)

Thomas Massaro, S.J.

The major motion picture *Selma*, which premiered on Christmas Day 2014, was a most timely contribution to American public life on two counts. First, it was released just months before the fiftieth anniversary of the enactment of the landmark Voting Rights Act of 1965. The availability of this film, the first major studio release ever to portray the figure of Dr. Martin Luther King Jr., as the central character of a drama, allowed generations of viewers to appreciate the enormous significance of the events in Selma, Alabama, and elsewhere that culminated in this momentous legislation that enacted key principles of social justice and reflected many of the core concerns of Catholic social teaching.

Thomas Massaro, S.J., is the Dean of the Jesuit School of Theology of Santa Clara University. A Jesuit priest with roots in New York and Boston, he was professor of moral theology for 15 years at Weston Jesuit School of Theology in Cambridge, Massachusetts, and at Boston College before arriving in Berkeley, California, in 2012 to become dean of JST-SCU. Father Massaro holds a doctorate in Christian social ethics from Emory University and is the author of several books and dozens of scholarly as well as popular articles devoted to Catholic social teaching and its recommendations for public policies oriented to social justice, peace, worker rights, and poverty alleviation.

Even before Dr. King (played so superbly on screen by David Oyelowo) enters the action of the film, the iconic actress Oprah Winfrey makes a bid to steal the show. The opening scenes of *Selma* present a microcosm of the wider canvas on which the drama of the struggle for voting rights is played out. The setting for this "miniature within the movie" is a county courthouse in Alabama, where one of the two characters in the scene (Winfrey's Annie Lee Cooper) anxiously approaches the other, a white male who is the clerk of the local electoral commission. Despite her most valiant effort and evident assiduous preparation for the task, the middle-aged African American woman is unable to complete her attempt to register to vote. The wily and clearly racist clerk erects barrier after barrier to Cooper's quest, including administering a political knowledge quiz that no mortal could pass—all in a spirited effort to frustrate the good-faith attempt of this granddaughter of chattel slaves to exercise her constitutional right. The Fourteenth Amendment, which had been wrested from centuries of racist practices by means of the sacrifices of Union soldiers wielding guns and bayonets, appears (at least temporarily) powerless before the power of a callous civil servant wielding a rubber stamp to deny the application. The remainder of the film relates the stony path by which this great injustice, and millions more like it, comes to be overturned at last.

Or is it overturned at last? The second reason why the film *Selma* is so timely involves an ongoing struggle against forces that threaten to roll back the gains of yesteryear regarding the right of all eligible citizens to vote. Sometimes called voter suppression, or euphemistically "anti-fraud measures to insure balloting integrity," pernicious efforts to curtail the ability of certain demographic groups to cast ballots in local, state, and national elections have been growing by leaps and bounds in recent years. Contemporary threats of disenfranchisement are decidedly more subtle than the dastardly maneuverings of a crafty county clerk, much less the violence unleashed by members of the Ku Klux Klan to harm or intimidate targets of their hatred. In the 21st century, systematic structural barriers that prevent members of minority groups from casting their ballots have replaced the personal callousness of a villain like this electoral official.

SUSPICIOUS PRACTICES, ASYMMETRICAL EFFECTS

Like so many shameful practices, voter suppression has its defenders and apologists. In some states, election officials have justified the adoption of new restrictive voter identification measures by pointing to the risk of fraud at the ballot box. Repeated studies have documented with irrefutable evidence how vanishingly rare voter fraud actually is; all those credibly accused of practicing voter fraud nationwide in most years could fit into a small elevator together. Nevertheless, in thinly veiled attempts to rationalize this injustice, some officials have continued to advance dubious solutions to a problem (impersonation at the polls) that seems hardly to exist. They have implemented unreasonably strict requirements to establish legal residency and eligibility to vote. Applicants face enhanced scrutiny to verify their identity and immigration status, and months before the next election must produce multiple forms of identification before they can enroll as voters.

Particularly pernicious are the asymmetrical effects of enhanced voting registration requirements, which have a way of sorting the privileged from the under-resourced. When registering to vote becomes a hassle, a disproportionate number of those with the time and resources to comply with enhanced requirements are the more affluent citizens, who are generally better prepared to negotiate the bureaucratic maze to eventual success. They are the fortunate ones who will likely cast ballots in the next election. What might constitute a slight annoyance to them is often a deep hardship for low-income people, a disproportionate number of whom are people of color, who face exclusion from the voting booth. Less affluent citizens often cannot take time off from work to visit county courthouses during business hours, or have trouble finding easy transportation to visit the required offices to produce a birth certificate, or encounter more difficulties in rounding up the necessary paperwork (such as utility bills, driver's licenses, or state-issued ID cards) which is often expensive to obtain.

It might be easy to cast blame on less affluent aspiring voters for their own plight in this regard, but moralizing about the situation does nothing to address the unmistakable problem and the resulting disparities. In fact, this same dynamic by which participation in the electoral system is discouraged by increased levels of bureaucratic requirements is quite familiar to social service workers. In just about every government benefit program, a surprisingly small percentage of those eligible actually receive the benefits to which they are entitled, simply because bureaucratic barriers (by design or not) discourage so many from applying or persevering toward a successful resolution. In some states, the "take-up rate" (as it is called) for nutrition and housing assistance is so low that the public programs barely make an impact on demonstrated human need for the essentials of life.

It is of course somewhat perilous to make generalizations about voter suppression, since every state—and often smaller jurisdictions within a given state, such as counties and municipalities—has its own regulations as well as its own recent experience and policy history. We have certainly come a long way from the time of the post-Reconstruction Black Codes and the Jim Crow system in the South, when blacks were systematically excluded from voting by means of rather blatant measures like poll taxes and literacy tests. In some states, voting has actually become easier in recent years, as "motor voter" provisions have made registering to vote a relatively simple process that is initiated as part of the driver's license application or renewal. (This of course does not address the challenges for non-drivers, who are in the aggregate among the least affluent.) Similarly, some states have joined the movement toward easier enrollment for absentee and mail-in ballots, so that those who do successfully register to vote need not visit polling places at all, or at least not on a busy Election Day itself, and may cast ballots in advance through the postal system. Early voting periods are additional measures that actually serve to increase voter turnout where they are in effect.

But it often seems that for every step toward ease of voting in one jurisdiction, another state or locality introduces restrictions that make it harder to register in the first place or to cast one's vote even after successful registration. At least a dozen states, including Indiana, Alabama, Florida, Kansas, and Texas, have introduced novel measures in recent years that will serve to discourage voters and depress voter turnout. For example, the state of Wisconsin was challenged in a case that is destined for the U.S. Supreme Court over the imposition of a requirement that voters would have to present photo IDs at the polling place each time they attempt to vote. It was no mere urban legend that so many voters in recent elections waited in unconscionably long lines—and of course some turned away because of the lengthy waiting times—because of understaffing at the polling place.

While it is always difficult to discern whether deliberate intentions lie behind observable behaviors like delays and confusion at the polls, the pattern whereby many potential voters are frustrated in their attempt to cast a ballot—and most of these in areas where low-income Americans tend to live—is very disturbing. Just imagine the deep frustration experienced by a hopeful voter turned away brusquely from the registration table in advance of an election or from the actual voting place on the day of an election suspecting that arbitrary or even hostile administrative maneuvers explain the denial of his or her attempt to vote. Proving that discriminatory intentions lie behind subtle forms of voter suppression is hard, but the discriminatory effect is real and obvious. The outcome is the locking out of the electoral system of a disproportionate number of low-income Americans—people who are more likely to vote in ways that are at odds with the preferences of the election officials designing and implementing the rules. Nobel laureate Joseph E. Stiglitz, in his 2014 volume *The Price of Inequality: How Today's Divided Society Endangers Our Future*, refers to these underhanded practices which chip away at voter participation in our democracy as "disenfranchisement by stealth." As such, unequal access to the voting rights that all citizens are entitled to is worthy of our full attention. It certainly deserves a higher profile than it typically receives in the U.S. mainstream media.

PRINCIPLES, LAWS AND RELIGIOUS ADVOCACY

Voter suppression is an offense against the key principle of equality before the law, which the Fourteenth Amendment enshrines in its landmark phrase "the equal protection of the laws." By threatening to deny access to one of the key rights of citizenship to those least able to advocate for themselves, practices that discourage or disallow voting by members of certain demographic groups call into question the very foundation of our identity as a democratic society. Free and fair access to voting is a precondition of true democracy, which is a fitting label only for societies that allow the voices of everyone to be heard. If a segment of the legitimate electorate is shortchanged or systematically under-represented, the shaping of our priorities through the electoral process will invariably be warped and distorted. All of our collective actions will come under suspicion—indeed, they well deserve to suffer under a cloud of suspicion until corrective measures are taken that level the playing field and restore proper order.

In other words, we should not be satisfied with our electoral system until it fully measures up to these words from the Fifteenth Amendment of the U.S. Constitution, which was ratified in 1870: "The right of citizens of the United States to vote shall not be denied or abridged by the United States or by any State on account of race, color, or previous condition of servitude."

The motion picture *Selma* captures a key moment in our nation's progress toward this goal. Its final scenes contain a panorama of the glorious effects of the passage of the Voting Rights Act, including a brief glimpse of Oprah Winfrey's character Annie Lee Cooper at last exercising her right to cast a ballot. So deeply moving is the portrayal of this triumph over the frustration and injustice that was captured in the opening scene of the movie that spontaneous applause broke out in the Bay Area theater where I viewed the film.

Ideally, we should not have to re-win over and over again the noble fight to secure voting rights for all. Regrettably, it appears that vigilance against voter suppression is still necessary, even urgent, if we are to stand up for the marginalized. Ever since it was enacted in 1965, the Voting Rights Act has ostensibly prohibited a wide range of voter suppression tactics, such as the erection of inordinate hurdles to voting in minority jurisdictions. However, simply having well-intentioned laws on the books is not enough. Also required is a committed group of advocates to keep our nation's practices fair and honest.

It is not hard to identify the most promising source of advocacy for overcoming unfair barriers to voting today. Religious communities have long been the most reliable and dedicated defenders of the rights of the marginalized in American society. Despite their own checkered history of regrettable blind spots that have at times prevented full-throated advocacy of the dispossessed, churches, mosques, synagogues and other houses of worship are key loci of social justice activism, as the film *Selma* portrays with its dramatic images of religious leaders leading the protest march across the Edmund Pettus Bridge on "Bloody Sunday" (March 7, 1965). Drawing upon their traditions' commitment to human dignity and human rights, our nation's religious communities are among the most prominent advocates of fair treatment for those threatened with disenfranchisement by current techniques of voter suppression.

The Roman Catholic tradition, with its particular orientation toward the common good and special regard for the poor and vulnerable, is especially well positioned to advocate for reforms that will counter these disturbing trends. A recent turn in Catholic theology—even before the election of Pope Francis, but with renewed vigor in the years since—urges greater sensitivity to the voices of the poor. Since it is generally low-income Americans and disproportionately members of ethnic minorities who most often face disenfranchisement in this way, it would be most fitting for the Catholic community to take the lead as a vocal advocate of fairer practices in voter registration and election procedures. If we want to see minority voters accorded their full constitutional rights, Catholic leaders—and especially the moral teachers who hold the office of bishop—will have to prioritize the cause of voting fairness.

CONSCIENCE, MISSIONARY DISCIPLESHIP, AND A CHURCH FOR THE POOR

DAVID E. DeCOSSE

San Diego Bishop Robert W. McElroy's noted essay "A Church for the Poor"[1] argues that the Catholic Church in the United States should undergo a conversion of heart and focus far more on the plight of the poor. I find McElroy's argument convincing, but I also think his essay implicitly raises a crucial, related question: Is the theology of conscience now in predominant use by the bishops of the United States adequate to such a task of conversion? In this essay, I will argue that it is not. In its place, I will offer instead the theology of conscience favored by Pope Francis as a more fruitful possibility for fostering the conversion to become a "church for the poor."

Of course, Francis has said that a concern for the poor is the key mark of authenticity of the church.[2] He has also often articulated principles of Catholic social doctrine in ways that re-invigorate the identity of the church as both poor in itself and dedicated to justice and mercy for the poor.[3] To be sure, Francis' understanding of the church and of

David E. DeCosse is the Director of Campus Ethics Programs at the Markkula Center for Applied Ethics at Santa Clara University, where he is also Adjunct Associate Professor of Religious Studies. He has written for academic journals like *Theological Studies* and journalistic outlets like *National Catholic Reporter*. With Kristin Heyer, he co-edited the book *Conscience and Catholicism: Rights, Responsibilities, and Institutional Responses* (Orbis 2015).

its principles of social doctrine will no doubt affect whether American Catholics are moved to become a church for the poor. But the way that we understand the theology of conscience will affect the possibility of such a transformation. One way of posing the challenge is to say: Can the Catholic Church in the United States move from its use of a theology of conscience oriented to abstract truth to a theology of conscience shaped by concrete persons?

FAITHFUL CITIZENSHIP AND THE FORMATION OF CONSCIENCE

For the last several years, the issue of the role of conscience in the American Catholic engagement with politics has been especially informed by the document called *Forming Consciences for Faithful Citizenship* (or *Faithful Citizenship*) published in each national election cycle by the United States Conference of Catholic Bishops. In it, the American Catholic bishops have drawn on the theology of conscience developed by the like-minded papacies of John Paul II and Benedict XVI.[4] In the view of these popes, the conscience of the Catholic citizen, in principle, was free to vote as she or he saw best. However, this was a sharply circumscribed freedom. On the one hand, in a favored locution of the last decades in the church, one has a free conscience but such a conscience must be properly formed. Moreover, *Faithful Citizenship* emphasizes the central and pre-eminent role of "church teaching" in the formation of conscience. Still more, the conscience of the Catholic citizen ought especially to know and oppose both actions that are intrinsically evil (e.g., abortion or actions motivated by racism) and laws and policies perceived as permitting such evils. To be sure, *Faithful Citizenship* encourages the formation of conscience in light of a broad range of principles articulated by John Paul II and Benedict XVI: the preferential option for the poor; solidarity; subsidiarity; the duty of caring for creation; and more. But the document is especially concerned to defend the Catholic conscience facing the threatened status of moral truth especially evident in issues of sexual ethics. And one of the surest signs of the cultural contempt for such truth is the pervasive neglect in citizens' conscience of the binding nature of the universal, objective, negative commandments (i.e., those commandments that pertain to intrinsic evils) that, for instance, prohibit the direct taking of the life of the innocent or the use of artificial birth control. The conscience of the Catholic citizen cannot be given a free pass in such a relativist, subjectivist culture.

In all of this, the theology of conscience in *Faithful Citizenship* stands squarely in line with the distinctive turn in the last two papacies away from key aspects of the theology of conscience articulated at the Second Vatican Council. At the heart of this turn is a preoccupation with the authority of the hierarchical church and with the self-evident clarity (self-evident to those wishing to see) of abstract moral truth. An example demonstrates this turning: *Faithful Citizenship* follows the usage of those papacies and insists that Catholics "form" their consciences in accord with Church teaching.[5] The word "form" suggests conforming: A strict alignment of conscience to the moral directives of the Magisterium. But in writing the *Declaration on Religious Freedom* at the Second Vatican Council, the council fathers specifically rejected this way of proceeding. They rejected the word "form" and instead, in a spirit more open to prudence, said that the Christian faithful in educating their consciences *"ought carefully to attend* to the sacred and certain doctrine of the Church" (emphasis added).[6]

McElroy's essay argues that the American bishops' emphasis on combatting intrinsic evils has become an obstacle to becoming a church for the poor. But how can the church in the United States move to a theology of conscience more attuned to the poor? The thought of Pope Francis offers a way of answering this question.

CONSCIENCE AND PERSONS

In his noted open letter in the fall of 2013 to Italian atheist and newspaperman Eugenio Scalfari, Pope Francis retrieved a Catholic tradition of the primacy of conscience disfavored during the preceding two papacies. In response to Scalfari's question about the possibility of Christian forgiveness for a person who neither believes nor seeks God, Francis said:

> The question for one who doesn't believe in God lies in obeying one's conscience. Sin, also for those who don't have faith, exists when one goes

against one's conscience. To listen to and to obey it means, in fact, to decide in face of what is perceived as good or evil.[7]

In recovering such a tradition, Francis has gone backward in order to go forward. While *Faithful Citizenship* stands in line with John Paul II and Benedict in its wariness of the subjectivism of conscience, Francis returns to key documents of the Second Vatican Council (and, before them, to Thomas Aquinas' 13th century writing on conscience) to signal a greater openness to the possibility of the sincere if mistaken conscience.[8] With Francis, the burden of proof has shifted: The judgment of conscience contrary to Catholic doctrine is less likely presumed to be culpably ignorant and more likely presumed, in the older language of moral theology, to be sincere if "invincibly ignorant."

In itself, Francis' more welcome view of the subjective nature of conscience does not link conscience to concern for the poor. But it signals an important shift that clears the way to begin moving in that direction. First, Francis is putting forward a view of conscience more consistent with the assumption that the church ought to be in dialogue with the world—about the problems of poverty and about other things, too. Many who may sharply disagree with the church on matters of civil law related to sexual ethics may do so with a sincere, mistaken, but not culpably malicious conscience. Many such groups could also be helpful allies in a battle against poverty and no longer need to pass litmus tests of moral purity mandated in the last years by conservative Catholic groups.[9] In any case, such a dialogical spirit is both a theological imperative of the church and a practical necessity for political engagement in a liberal, pluralist society like the United States. Second, Francis is advancing a view of conscience that favors the inner life of persons over the outer demands of moral abstractions. Conscience formation reduced primarily to concerns about intrinsic evils fails to do justice to the complex, relational, and deeply personal nature of conscience itself.

Shortly before becoming pope, Cardinal Ratzinger had argued: "The decline of a moral conscience grounded in absolute values is still our problem today."[10] By contrast, Francis in his interview with Scalfari rejected any notion of absolute truth insofar as the "absolute is what is inconsistent, what is deprived of any relationship."[11] Truth, he said, is best understood as a relationship. Or, in another way of putting it, he said that truth is one with love and thus one with the way we seek, receive, and express the truth of another person—and especially the person of Jesus Christ. Moreover, Francis added, we understand truth only in the context of our history and culture. We understand others' truth only by seeking out and appreciating the context of their history and culture. Here the theme of missionary discipleship that is central to Francis' papacy provides a helpful interpretive key. It is not only— to use the drier philosophical language of the previous papacies—that our conscience's grasp of truth depends on the quality of our moral character. But it is also that the bold, proactive spirit of missionary discipleship seeks out the poor and, amid the exercise of prudence in such a context, fosters the formation of conscience in moral truth. He powerfully explained this process of conscience formation in a speech in Bolivia to community activists:

> This rootedness in the barrio, the land, the office, the labor union, this ability to see yourselves in the faces of others, this daily proximity to their share of troubles and their little acts of heroism: this is what enables you to practice the commandment of love, not on the basis of ideas or concepts, but rather on the basis of genuine interpersonal encounter. We do not love concepts or ideas; we love people… Commitment, true commitment, is born of the love of men and women, of children and the elderly, of peoples and communities…of names and faces which fill our hearts.[12]

CONSCIENCE AND THE CHURCH

In *Faithful Citizenship*, conscience is conservative in the sense of conserving moral truth. Cardinal Ratzinger provided a strong push toward such a tendency when in a noted essay he argued that "anamnesis" or memory was the best way of understanding the fundamental drive of conscience toward the good and away from evil: The drive is protective of the moral truth handed down over generations and written into our very being by the creative act of God.[13] Moreover, *Faithful Citizenship* is written with the spirit of strong conviction that the hierarchical teaching office of the church knows what this truth is and knows what every Catholic conscience should know. Or, as John Paul said in *Veritatis splendor*: "...the Magisterium does not bring to the Christian conscience truths which are extraneous to it; rather it brings to light the truths which it ought already to possess."[14] To be sure, *Faithful Citizenship* is not uniformly dedicated to conservation. In the document, the bishops note John Paul's admonition that it is as important to do good as it is not to do evil. But, overall, the sense of *Faithful Citizenship* is wary: The church is a sentinel holding a defensive line in a culture war.

With Pope Francis, however, conscience is oriented more clearly toward prudential possibilities for doing the good, not to obediential demands for keeping the law. In his discussion in *Evangelii Gaudium* of the church's millennia-long concern for the poor, he says: "We should not be concerned simply about falling into doctrinal error, but about remaining faithful to this light-filled path of life and wisdom."[15] Along with the drive of missionary discipleship, several additional factors in Francis' theology turn conscience toward the good and the future. One is the importance and immediacy of the connection between conscience and the *deus semper maior*, the "always greater God," or—in a favorite phrase of Francis—the "God of surprises."[16] Here Francis recalls the emphasis of St. Ignatius of Loyola on the immediacy of the relationship between the soul and God. Here Francis also recalls the transcendent dimension of conscience articulated in the Second Vatican Council's *Gaudium et Spes* (where a person "is alone with God"[17]). By thinking of conscience in this way, Francis opens space between conscience and the hierarchical teaching office that was tightly closed in the last decades: The fundamental orientation of conscience is to God, not to the Magisterium. Moreover, Francis also allows for the creative dimension of conscience—creative not because all by itself conscience comes up with new things (a great fear of John Paul and Benedict) but because the God of surprises reveals new things to the conscience fired with the love of missionary discipleship.

An additional theological factor helps to link the creative potential of conscience to the poor. Key here is Francis' insistence on the church as the whole people of God, hierarchy and laity together possessing an instinct for the truth of doctrine and practice. In a church imagined in this way, the formation of conscience is not exclusively top-down. Instead, conscience emerges more clearly as shaped by the vast, vibrant social dynamic of the people of God living in a world of prudence, ritual, service, friendship, prayer, sacrament, image, and more. And, for Francis, the poor have a crucial role to play in this horizontal process of the *sensus fidelium*. As he said: "This is why I want a Church which is poor and for the poor. They [the poor] have much to teach us .... We need to let ourselves be evangelized by them."[18]

In conclusion, Bishop McElroy has called for the church in the United States to be a church for the poor. Accordingly, it is time for the Catholic bishops of the United States to update *Faithful Citizenship* with a Pope Francis-inspired theology of conscience more fitting for that task.

1 Robert W. McElroy, "A Church for the Poor," *America* magazine (October 23, 2013). Bishop McElroy's essay is reprinted in this volume.

2 Pope Francis, Apostolic Exhortation on the Proclamation of the Gospel Today, *Evangelii Gaudium* (2013), 195. Cited hereafter as EG.

3 Ibid, 198.

4 For the discussion of conscience in the Unites States Conference of Catholic Bishops, *Forming Consciences for Faithful Citizenship* (2011) http://www.usccb.org/issues-and-action/faithful-citizenship/forming-consciences-for-faithful-citizenship-document.cfm, see paragraphs 17-39 (and especially 17-18). See also John Paul II, Encyclical Regarding Certain Fundamental Questions of the Church's Moral Teaching, *Veritatis Splendor* (1993), 54-64 (Cited hereafter as VS) and Joseph Ratzinger, "Conscience and Truth," in *Crisis of Conscience*, ed. John M. Haas (New York: Crossroad, 1996), 2-20.

5 *Faithful Citizenship*, 17.

6 Second Vatican Council, Declaration on Religious Freedom, *Dignitatis Humanae* (1965), 14. See also Gregory Kalscheur, S.J., "Conscience and Citizenship: The Primacy of Conscience for Catholics in Public Life," *Journal of Social Thought* 6:2 (2009): 327-329.

7 "Pope Francis' Letter to the Founder of *La Repubblica* Italian Newspaper," *Zenit* (September 11, 2013), accessed July 20, 2015, http://www.zenit.org/en/articles/pope-francis-letter-to-the-founder-of-la-repubblica-italian-newspaper.

8 See, for instance, Thomas Aquinas, *Summa Theologica* I-II, Question 19, Article 5: "Whether the Will is Evil When It Is at Variance with Erring Reason."

9 See John Gehring, "Be Not Afraid: Guilt by Association, Catholic McCarthyism, and Growing Threats to the U.S. Bishops' Anti-Poverty Mission," *Faith in Public Life* (2013), accessed on July 20, 2015, http://www.faithinpubliclife.org/wp-content/uploads/2013/06/FPL-CCHD-report.pdf.

10 Joseph Ratzinger, "The Spiritual Roots of Europe: Yesterday, Today, Tomorrow," in *Without Roots: The West, Relativism, Christianity, Islam.* Trans. Michael F. Moore (New York: Basic Books, 2006), 74.

11 "Pope Francis' Letter to the Founder of *La Repubblica*."

12 "Read Pope Francis' Speech on the Poor and Indigenous Peoples," *Time*, July 10, 2015, accessed on July 20, 2105, http://time.com/3952885/pope-francis-bolivia-poverty-speech-transcript/.

13 Ratzinger, "Conscience and Truth," 13.

14 VS, 64.

15 EG, 194.

16 Pope Francis in an interview with Antonio Spadaro, "A Big Heart Open to God," *America Magazine* (September 30, 2013).

17 The Second Vatican Council, Pastoral Constitution on the Church in the Modern World, *Gaudium et Spes* (1965), 16.

18 EG, 198.

APPENDIX:
A CHURCH FOR THE POOR

ROBERT W. MCELROY

'How many poor people there still are in the world! And what great suffering they have to endure!" With these words the new pope explained to international diplomats assembled at the Vatican on March 22 why he chose the name Francis at the moment of his election. And since then Pope Francis has unswervingly pointed to the scandal of poverty in a world of plenty as a piercing moral challenge for the church and the whole human community.

In part, the pope's message has called us to personal conversion, speaking powerfully to each of us about how we let patterns of materialism captivate our lives and distort our humanity. In a disarming way, Francis seeks to make us all deeply uncomfortable, so that in our discomfort we may recognize and confront the alienation from our own humanity that occurs when we seek happiness in objects rather than in relationship with God and others.

Francis' message also has been an invitation to cultural conversion, laying bare the three false cultures that materialism has created in our world: the culture of comfort that makes us think only of ourselves;

Most Rev. Robert W. McElroy at the time of this publication was auxiliary bishop of San Francisco. On March 3, 2015, he was appointed bishop of San Diego. Reprinted from *America*, October 21, 2013, with permission of America Press, Inc., 2013. All rights reserved. For subscription information, call 1-800-627-9533 or visit www.americamedia.org.

the culture of waste that seizes the gifts of the created order only to savor them for a moment and then discard them; and the culture of indifference that desensitizes us to the suffering of others, no matter how intense, no matter how sustained. Pope Francis' words about the "globalization of indifference" echo the poignant observation of Pope Benedict in his encyclical "Charity in Truth" (2009): "As society becomes ever more globalized, it makes us neighbors but does not make us brothers."

And finally, the pope's message has been one of structural reform in the world. In June Francis explained: "A way has to be found to enable everyone to benefit from the fruits of the earth, and not simply to close the gap between the affluent and those who must be satisfied with the crumbs falling from the table." Francis has made clear that the present economic slowdown cannot be an excuse for inaction. Rather, there must immediately commence "a new stimulus to international activity on behalf of the poor, inspired by something more than mere goodwill, or, worse, promises which all too often have not been kept."

Pope Francis' teachings on the rights of the poor have enormous implications for the culture and politics of the United States and for the church in this country. Both the substance and methodology of Pope Francis' teachings on the rights of the poor have enormous implications for the culture and politics of the United States and for the church in this country. These teachings demand a transformation of the existing Catholic political conversation in our nation, a transformation reflecting three themes: prioritizing the issue of poverty, focusing not only on intrinsic evils but also on structural sin, and acting with prudence when applying Catholic moral principles to specific legal enactments.

PRIORITIZE POVERTY

The depth of the moral responsibility of the United States to fight global poverty arises from the tremendous power that our country exerts in the world economy. More than any other nation, the United States has the capacity to influence trading relationships, the availability of capital, and market conditions. If Francis' vision of a world with truly just trading and financial structures is to be realized, then the United

States and Europe must take a leading role in reforming the existing rules that so often victimize incipient markets in staggeringly poor countries.

In addition, the United States and the richest nations of the world community have a moral responsibility to share from their plenty with the poorest peoples in the human family. In 2002 the wealthy nations of the world pledged to direct 0.7 percent of their gross domestic product toward the alleviation of dire poverty by the year 2015. This level of investment would largely eliminate severe poverty on the planet. However, the United States and most of the other leading economic powers have reneged on their commitment; today the United States only gives 0.2 percent of its gross domestic product in development assistance. As a result, millions of children die each year from disease and malnutrition that could be prevented. This is social sin, arising from individual decisions. This is the visible presence of a "global culture of indifference" that lets us avert our eyes while our governments consciously make choices to reinforce our culture of comfort while ignoring the countless human lives lost as a consequence.

Within the United States, we also turn our eyes away from the growing domestic inequality that ruins lives and breaks spirits. Pope Francis speaks directly to this: "While the income of a minority is increasing exponentially, that of the majority is crumbling. This imbalance results from ideologies which uphold the absolute autonomy of markets and financial speculation, and thus deny the right of control to States, which are themselves charged with providing for the common good." The United States, which for so much of its great history has stood for economic mobility and a broad, comfortable middle class, now reflects gross disparities in income and wealth and barriers to mobility. The poor suffer a "benign neglect" in our political conversations, and absorb brutal cuts in governmental aid, especially at the state level.

If the Catholic Church is truly to be a "church for the poor" in the United States, it must elevate the issue of poverty to the very top of its political agenda, establishing poverty alongside abortion as the pre-eminent moral issues the Catholic community pursues at this moment in our nation's history. Both abortion and poverty countenance the deaths of millions of children in a world where government action could end the slaughter. Both abortion and poverty, each in its own way and to its own degree, constitute an assault on the very core of the dignity of the human person, instrumentalizing life as part of a throwaway culture. The cry of the unborn and the cry of the poor must be at the core of Catholic political conversation in the coming years because these realities dwarf other threats to human life and dignity that confront us today.

STRUCTURAL SIN

Another part of the needed transformation in Catholic political conversation is a renewed focus on structural sin. In pursuing many vital elements of the common good, structural sin is actually more relevant than sins of intrinsic evil.

The Catechism of the Catholic Church defines the common good as "the sum total of social conditions which allow people, either as groups or as individuals, to reach their fulfillment fully and more easily." There are three elements in the common good: respect for the fundamental and inalienable rights of the human person, the social well being and development of society, and the stability and security of a just order. The common good is primarily accomplished by the variety of social institutions—family, religious communities, economic enterprises, labor unions, and service organizations—that lie outside of government. But a crucial element of the common good falls to government for its realization. John Courtney Murray, S.J., called this element "the public order."

The mission of the Catholic community within the public order in the United States is to move in a comprehensive way to focus government on the enhancement of human rights, the development of society, and social peace. Part of that movement must address issues of intrinsic evil—acts that can never be justified regardless of intentions and circumstances—like murder, genocide, abortion, euthanasia, racism, torture, suicide, and slavery.

Intrinsically evil acts are always and everywhere wrong, but not all intrinsically evil acts fall within the scope of the public order and the role of government. Intrinsically evil acts like adultery and blasphemy are always wrong, but they do not lie within the jurisdiction of government. Some intrinsically evil acts, like racism, lie partly within the scope of government and partly outside. Racial discrimination in housing or unemployment must be legally proscribed, but contemptible racism expressed in private conversation generally should not. Finally, there are acts of intrinsic evil so grave and so contrary to the role of law in society that opposition to them is absolutely central to the Catholic mission of seeking the common good. Abortion and euthanasia are such issues because they involve the most fundamental duty of government to prevent the taking of innocent human life.

It is crucial to fully recognize the nature of intrinsic evil and its relationship to the common good. In recent years, however, some arguments have been broadly advanced in Catholic political conversation proposing that issues pertaining to intrinsically evil acts automatically have priority in the public order over all other issues of grave evil, like poverty, war, unjust immigration laws, and the lack of restorative justice in the criminal justice system. This has the effect of labeling these other crucial issues of Catholic social teaching "optional" in the minds of many Catholics.

The statements of Pope Francis on poverty demonstrate why issues of intrinsic evil do not automatically have priority in advancing the common good. The category of intrinsic evil is vital in identifying the exceptionless evil inherent in certain types of actions. Poverty, however, is not a one-time action. It is the result of countless specific human actions with varying degrees of responsibility that give rise to social structures and practices imbued with selfishness and evil. The category of intrinsic evil cannot capture the type of entrenched evil inherent in poverty. Yet Francis clearly teaches that alleviating the grave evil of poverty must be at the very heart of the church's mission. It is neither optional nor secondary.

Like war, the exploitation of undocumented immigrants and our distorted system of criminal justice, poverty is a structural sin rooted

121

in the very life of society and government. Structural sin constitutes the effect of personal sins that collectively create social situations and institutions fundamentally opposed to divine goodness.

Pope Francis attested poignantly to the reality and the impersonality of structural sin when he visited Lampedusa, where hundreds of undocumented immigrants died in a shipwreck while seeking a new life in Italy. "Who is responsible for the blood of these brothers and sisters of ours?" Francis asked. "Nobody! That is our answer. It isn't me; I don't have anything to do with it; it must be someone else, but certainly not me. Yet God is asking each of us: 'Where is the blood of your brother that cries out to me?'"

Some essential elements for advancing the common good pertain to opposing intrinsically evil acts. Some pertain to issues of structural sin. And others, as "The Splendor of Truth" (1993) reminds us, fall under the category of accomplishing great goods, like the profoundly beautiful vision of social solidarity advanced by Pope John Paul II or the pioneering reflections on stewardship and creation that Pope Benedict XVI brought to the world. There is no single category of sin or evil, social good or virtue, that is the filter for discerning the priorities of the church in the public order. The concept of the common good is multidimensional in its very nature, and any reductionist effort to minimize this quality is a distortion of our heritage and teaching.

ROLE OF PRUDENCE

The role of prudence has been one of the most misused elements in the Catholic political conversation in the United States in recent years. It is frequently asserted, particularly in election years, that issues pertaining to intrinsic evils do not necessitate prudential judgment, while other grave evils like war, poverty, or the unjust treatment of immigrants are merely prudentially laden issues on which people of good will can disagree.

The truth is that prudence is a necessary element of any effort to advance the common good through governmental action. Moving from even the clearest moral principle to specific legislation or administrative action involves questions of strategy, prioritization, and practicality.

Even then, no law or program can ever encapsulate the clarity and fullness of the original moral principle.

Consider the issue of abortion, which represents probably the least complex application of clear and compelling Catholic moral principle to law. It is clear that Catholic teaching demands robust and effective legal sanctions against abortion. But should the law criminalize abortion for the mother or for those performing the abortion? Alternatively, should there be noncriminal sanctions? What is the best pathway to outlawing abortion: a series of graduated proposals beginning with parental notification and prohibitions on late-term abortion, or an immediate full-court press for comprehensive prohibitions? These are questions on which people of good will can disagree in full accord with Catholic teaching, since all of these approaches seek to achieve the core principle that the law should protect the life of the unborn. Thus this is wholly different from the candidate who refuses to vote for any legal restrictions on abortion and argues that he is in fact doing more to reduce abortions by his support for aid to the poor and health care programs. Such a candidate has rejected the core substance contained in the Catholic teaching on abortion and civil law.

The core teaching of the church on the role of government in combating poverty declares that in addition to promoting conditions that provide meaningful jobs for their citizens, nations must provide a humane threshold of income, health benefits, and housing. So it is with the issue of poverty. The core teaching of the church on the role of government in combating poverty declares that in addition to promoting conditions that provide meaningful jobs for their citizens, nations must provide a humane threshold of income, health benefits, and housing. Just as important, as Pope Francis has repeatedly taught, wealthy nations must work ardently to reduce gross inequalities of wealth within their borders and beyond. Accomplishing these goals requires a series of complex prudential decisions about financial structures, incentives for wealth creation, and income support programs that enhance rather than undermine family life. Many different types of choices are compatible within a full commitment to Catholic teachings on economic justice.

But choices by citizens or public officials that systematically, and therefore unjustly, decrease governmental financial support for the poor clearly reject core Catholic teachings on poverty and economic justice. Policy decisions that reduce development assistance to the poorest countries reject core Catholic teachings. Tax policies that increase rather than decrease inequalities reject core Catholic teachings. The nature and tone of Pope Francis' declarations on poverty and evil in the world powerfully convey that while prudence is necessary in the formulation of economically just policies, the categorical nature of Catholic teaching on economic justice is clear and binding.

The teachings of Pope Francis on "a church for the poor" not only speak to the centrality of addressing poverty as an imperative for Catholics in the public order, but also call us to look anew at the nature of the common good in society and how we seek to achieve it. We are called to see the issues of abortion and poverty, marriage and immigrant rights, euthanasia and war, religious liberty and restorative justice, not as competing alternatives often set within a partisan framework, but as a complementary continuum of life and dignity. We are called to create a Catholic political conversation that proclaims the greatest problems of our day can only be solved with a vision rooted in the transcendent dignity of the human person. For in the end, the very purpose of Catholic political conversations is to help our nation see human suffering and human striving not through the lens of politics but as God sees them.

CPSIA information can be obtained
at www.ICGtesting.com
Printed in the USA
BVOW08s1543201116
468421BV00001B/174/P